PLOTTING GIGANTIC WORX

THE STORY OF ELGAR'S APOSTLES TRILOGY

MICHAEL FOSTER

CITY OF BIRMINGHAM SYMPHONY ORCHESTRA
at
The Worcestershire Press

Text © Michael Foster 1995, 2003

Published in the United Kingdom by
The Worcestershire Press
Caves Farm, Chatley,
Droitwich, Worcestershire
WR9 0AP

Original specification by
Dr Derek Foxton Publishing, Hereford

Typesetting and origination by
Kearline Graphic Images, Newport, NP19 7EJ

Typeset in 11/14pt Venetian
Printed and bound in Great Britain by
The Amadeus Press, Cleckheaton, BD19 4TQ

British Library Cataloguing In Publication Data
Foster, Michael
Plotting Gigantic Worx - The Story of Elgar's Apostles Trilogy
I.   Oratorio
I.   Title
782.3232092

ISBN 0-9544197-0-7

Library of Congress Cataloguing In Publication Data applied for

Thames Publishing originally produced this book as *Elgar's Gigantic Worx* (ISBN 0-905210-79-4)
in collaboration with The Three Choirs Festival Association Ltd for a serial performance of *The
Apostles* and *The Kingdom* at the 1995 Gloucester Three Choirs Festival. The new edition has been
published in association with The City of Birmingham Symphony Orchestra & Chorus to celebrate
their centenary performances (together with the City of Birmingham Choir) of *The Apostles* at
Symphony Hall, Birmingham, in October 2003.

CONTENTS

ACKNOWLEDGEMENTS

When the first edition of this book was published in 1995, it had grown out of mainly unused material for my M.Phil thesis – *Elgar's Apostles Trilogy as a Symphonic Concept* (University of Wales College, Cardiff 1996) – and was intended as an introduction to *The Apostles* and *The Kingdom* for audiences at the Gloucester Three Choirs Festival that year. I had always intended to revise the book and am therefore grateful to the City of Birmingham Symphony Orchestra for allowing me the opportunity in connection with the centenary performances of *The Apostles*. Sakari Oramo, the CBSO's Music Director; Stephen Maddock, the CBSO's Chief Executive and Simon Halsey, the CBSO's Chorus Director have given me much support and encouragement.

My 1995 retracing of the painful journey Elgar made while writing the two completed works of the Apostles Trilogy acutely increased my awareness of the effect that time pressures have on creativity. Now, by allowing myself the luxury of a longer time-span to revise and rewrite the book, I have been able to call upon the expertise of others in testing out my ideas. Here I must express my particular thanks to David Threasher, Editorial Manager, BBC Proms Publications, for not only editing the text but also offering advice on my additions to the original book; to Catherine Panting, Head of Music at King Charles I School, Kidderminster, for her work on Elgar's libretto setting, cross-checking the appendices and offering advice on the format of the rewritten material, but especially for so much patient reassurance during a difficult time; to Dr. Derek Foxton for originally typesetting the manuscript, processing the illustrations, and his work on the specification of the finished book; to Jenny Taylor of Jay Tee Studio Designs, Ross-on-Wye, for designing the cover and working on the overall layout of the text and illustrations; to Catherine Sloan, Museum Director of the Elgar Birthplace Museum and her staff for help with illustrations and source material; to the staff of the Worcester County Records Office for their help with source material; to the Archive Department of the British Library for tracing and supplying illustrations from the original manuscripts in their possession; to the staff of the Music Reading Room at the Bodleian Library, University of Oxford for tracing and supplying illustrations from the original manuscripts in their possession; to Paul Taylor of the Local Studies & History Department, Birmingham Central Library for tracing and supplying illustrations from the Birmingham City Archive; to Jane Barnes, KopyKats Design & Print, Droitwich for her work in photocopying and binding the many manuscript rewrites – often at short notice, but always with good humour.

Discussions with Richard Hickox, Vernon Handley, Mark Elder and Adrian Lucas about aspects of their approach to conducting both *The Apostles* and *The Kingdom* have proved invaluable in expanding my ideas for Part Two of the book. The Archive Department at EMI Records have generously allowed me access to the notes made by Sir Adrian Boult for their recordings of *The Apostles* and *The Kingdom*. RCA have made similar material available from Leonard Slatkin's recording of *The Kingdom*. Dr Percy Young has, during our discussions, provided a unique insight into the way that Elgar's material for the unwritten oratorio of the Apostles Trilogy was used in the — eventually unfinished — opera *The Spanish Lady* (completed by Percy Young in 1995). During my work on revising the original book, Anthony Payne's 'realisation' of Elgar's Third Symphony was premiered. Our discussions about Elgar's sketches for his unfinished symphony, using material originally destined for the unwritten oratorio, have proved invaluable.

I am also grateful to Novello & Co for permission to reproduce the complete texts of *The Apostles* and *The Kingdom*. The words of the two oratorios reproduced in Part Two of the present book, however, represents only the text created by Elgar, but not laid out in accordance with his very strict instructions for the published scores.

Finally, my heartfelt thanks go to Maggie Callaghan for giving so much support and encouragement from the start of this project and through what became a very taxing time.

PICTURE CREDITS

Most of the photographs in this book have been supplied by the Elgar Birthplace Museum. I am, however, grateful to Birmingham Central Library for providing the image of August Jaeger and George Hope Johnston; to Dr Derek Foxton for the photograph of Ivor Atkins; to Harrison Parrott for Clive Barda's photograph of Sakari Oramo.

SAKARI ORAMO
Music Director of The City of Birmingham Symphony Orchestra

It had always been CBSO's intention to celebrate the centenaries of the three major choral works that Elgar wrote for the Birmingham Triennial Festival between 1900 and 1906. October 2000 saw our two critically acclaimed performances of *The Dream of Gerontius* and, as October 2003 approaches, we now turn our attention to *The Apostles*. Yet, in preparing this work, I am increasingly conscious of a responsibility to demonstrate for audiences what Elgar himself could never accept – that *The Apostles* is not a failure; that it points directly towards a mastery of the symphonic form which was to be his future direction.

Composers fascinate me and the process of composition is something that I, as a conductor, work hard at understanding. When it comes to Elgar's methods in *The Apostles* and *The Kingdom* I am more than ever amazed that out of the chaos, both creative *and* personal, which surrounded him at the time, we have two works of such great achievement. What the third oratorio would have produced can only be imagined. Creating his own libretto when the music was already fixed in his mind seems to have meant improvisation on the grandest scale. This high risk strategy was almost Elgar's downfall, yet the Wagnerian dimensions of the Apostles project at its finest surely prove that he was right to set out on this road.

Sir Adrian Boult, a distinguished predecessor of mine with the City of Birmingham [Symphony] Orchestra, was a passionate admirer of both *The Apostles* and *The Kingdom*. Indeed, he regarded parts of these works as surpassing *The Dream of Gerontius*. My study of them, however, tells me that comparisons are not really valuable as they are so different in concept. Yet in all three works Elgar shows himself to be a natural musician, gradually coming to terms with the unending curiosity of an intellect that was largely self-taught.

As Music Director of the City of Birmingham Symphony Orchestra, I welcome Michael Foster's book which explores, in an imaginative way, Elgar's struggles to create two highly original works. Performers and audiences alike will, I am sure, warm to this portrait of Elgar as a man trying to make sense of his beliefs and who never quite allowed himself enough time to realise the ultimate ambition of his creative life.

INTRODUCTION

Elgar's Apostles project – the concept of at least three oratorios on the founding of the early Christian Church – was perhaps his greatest temptation and his biggest gamble. The two works that were eventually composed represented, for him at least, a failure to achieve his vision and this sense of failure was to remain with Elgar to the end of his life. *The Apostles* contains about half the material detailed in the press during the spring of 1903, some six months before the first performance. It ends at the Ascension, which should have been the original conclusion only for the first part of the oratorio. With *The Kingdom* the same thing happened, leaving only the original first part. The scheme could never, seemingly, quite come together and as a result Elgar gave up on it. The Apostles project, however, remains unique in Elgar's output and in English music as a whole, with the possible exception of the operas by Rutland Boughton written on the Arthurian legend – *The Birth of Arthur, The Round Table, The Lily Maid, Galahad* and *Avalon*. No other British composer has attempted a series of works continuing a single story by cross-referencing their music in such a giant tapestry.

While it is clear that Elgar had been contemplating the vast sweep of the Apostles story for many years, perhaps since he was a child, nothing could come of it until he had established himself as an important composer. In the early years his composing went hand in hand with earning a living as a violin teacher, an orchestral player and working in his father's music shop. With the success of the *Variations on an Original Theme, 'Enigma'* Op. 36 in 1899, Elgar at last became established as a composer of national importance, and when he was offered the opportunity of composing a commissioned work for the 1900 Birmingham Triennial Music Festival his thoughts turned immediately to the long-cherished ambition of setting the Apostles story. Elgar was soon to realise that the work required more time than he had available and so, instead, set Cardinal Newman's poem *The Dream of Gerontius*.

Eventually *The Dream of Gerontius* became recognised for the masterpiece it was, which led to a further Birmingham Festival commission, this time for 1903. At last there appeared to be time to undertake his Apostles project, but without an adequate libretto writing even the first work became difficult. The original concept would have seen the initial oratorio end with the conversion of the Gentiles and the establishment of the early Christian Church. By June 1903 he realised that the work could not be completed in time for the festival, and left off composition after the Ascension scene. Elgar told his publisher: 'I have been seeing my London doctor and my eyes are again in trouble – he forbids more work: now I propose to the Birmingham people that they produce Parts I and II of the Apostles – this portion is complete in itself and may well stand alone . . . The concluding portion of the work – much of which was written first – you can have anytime later'.[1]

This was only partially true. The struggle that Elgar had to get even this work ready for the festival left him with an acute sense of failure which, together with other more personal matters, led him to the verge of a nervous breakdown.

The 'concluding portion' referred to by Elgar in 1903 was to become *The Kingdom,* written in response to a commission for the 1906 Birmingham Festival. The problems with this work were even more acute. The schedule became tighter and, overall, Elgar's health was much worse. Also, his friend and confidant August Jaeger, Publishing Manager at Novello & Company, was in Switzerland recovering from serious illness. Where he had supported the composer through the trauma of putting together *The Apostles,* others were called upon to help with *The Kingdom.* Outside the family this task fell to Alfred Littleton, Novello's Chairman, who had become a near neighbour of Elgar's in Hereford. Littleton, not always the most enthusiastic supporter of Elgar's seemingly haphazard composition methods, was able to stand in for Jaeger as much as possible during the new crisis over *The Kingdom.*

Lack of a libretto, together with other pressures of a professional and personal nature, led Elgar again to the verge of a nervous breakdown; he came very close to resigning the commission altogether. With support, the second oratorio was completed but once again fell far short of his expectations. Where it should have ended in a blaze of light with the establishment of the early Christian Church there was only the hushed finale of the Lord's Prayer completed years earlier. The work covered less than half the distance from the events he intended to portray in the very first oratorio of the scheme. No real hope remained then of the project's continuation. Elgar's pain over *The Apostles* and *The Kingdom* resulted in the end of his sacred choral music writing.

Although he returned again and again to the sketches, nothing more came of the great scheme. 1909 should have seen the trilogy completed for Birmingham but, perhaps wisely, no commission was offered. When Elgar's great friend Ivor Atkins did make an offer for the 1914 Three Choirs Festival it was refused on financial grounds. Elgar's skills had, in any event, turned to the symphonic form.

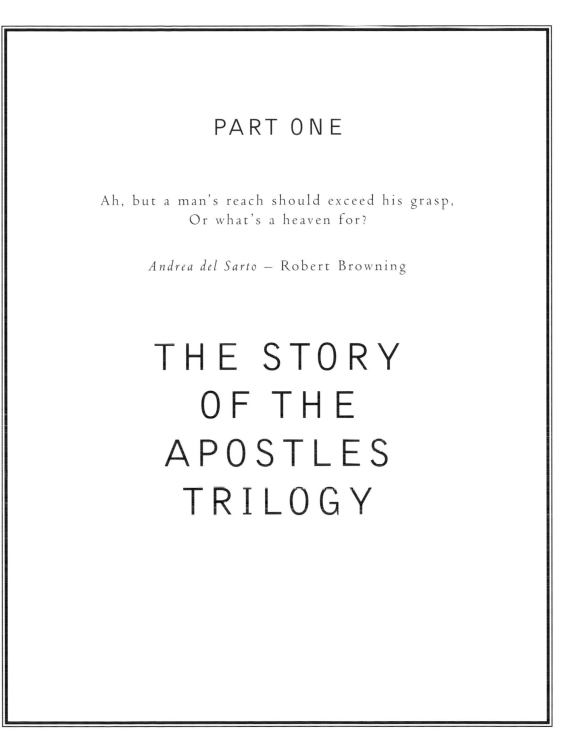

PART ONE

Ah, but a man's reach should exceed his grasp,
Or what's a heaven for?

Andrea del Sarto – Robert Browning

THE STORY OF THE APOSTLES TRILOGY

CHAPTER ONE

A CHALLENGE TO THE ALMIGHTY

Edward Elgar was brought up a Roman Catholic but in a far from ordinary Catholic family. His father was a freethinker without any structure of faith at all who became organist at the local Catholic church more on financial grounds than any other. His mother, though, was a cottage intellectual, a book collector and a great reader. For anyone – especially a woman – in a provincial city during the mid-19th century there were very few ways of opening the mind. While it could be argued that religion has the potential to close the mind, Catholicism offered Ann Elgar just what she wanted. She became a convert, raising her children in the same way, against her husband's opposition.

Elgar's early attitudes were shaped by the ancient traditions of the Church; attitudes which have been described as medieval, and which were certainly avidly mystical. Elgar was a Catholic – but perhaps not an entirely convinced one. In common with so many of his generation, the advance of science and technology served to unsettle the old certainties in his mind. But for Elgar, brought up in a household divided over religious imperatives, the conflict between 'medieval-renaissance' and 'romantic-classical' enthusiasms engendered a far greater sense of doubt than is the norm in the quest for spiritual truth. This was a conflict that remained unresolved to the end of his life. Therein, perhaps, lay the seat of his deepest unhappiness as well as of his genius.

His doubts had led him away from any kind of 'orthodoxy' while, perhaps initially, he still retained a very strong faith. This conundrum centred on his perception of religious professionals, not only in his own Church but also of every denomination. He regarded them as uncaring, slick and, from their secure ivory towers, much too prepared to ignore any kind of suffering and despair.

Elgar's mother and father in old age

Is it not therefore entirely possible that the appeal of the Apostles led him into a sort of divine challenge? By embarking on this epic story might not Elgar have been seeking the way back to faith? Might not the very nature of God be revealed to him? The subject was a limitless one because the Church, established as described in the Acts of the Apostles, continued to the end of the New Testament and beyond. Here was material enough for far more than one oratorio and perhaps enough to be used, one way or another, in the whole of Elgar's output. Was this the attraction? Or would a definite Biblical subject with a non-Catholic text (unlike *The Dream of Gerontius* which initially caused the composer such problems with complete performances in some ecclesiastical venues) have a wider appeal and be more acceptable to Anglican England?

His first thoughts were always of the music, and of the text somehow growing out of it, rather than the conscious setting of text to music. Such a universally accepted, divinely inspired story as that of Christ's Apostles and the establishment of the Christian Church would offer Elgar, for the first time, an opportunity, with some experienced help – preferably from respected Anglican theologians – to write his own libretto. He would not even have to use complete Biblical passages but could, by taking phrases and whole lines from diverse sources in both the New and Old Testaments, create a text to match exactly his requirements so long as the sense of the story remained. It is unclear whether Elgar was ever fully able to identify with the story itself, given his own spiritual doubts. But foremost among Biblical subjects, the Apostles story had, at its heart, the inspiration of ordinary human beings by a divine power beyond themselves. This was the promise that had lasted for almost two thousand years. This was the temptation. The last judgement had not yet come; the story was still going on.

But if the story he set out to tell was limitless, which of the characters in it would emerge as the 'hero'? Would that person ultimately have to prove himself more powerful than Christ, in whose name the Church was founded? It was here surely that his thoughts must have turned to Judas, the most unsympathetic character in the whole story. Yet Judas always was Elgar's man and he understood his character intimately. Although the way Elgar eventually portrayed Judas was unconventional, this figure above all others could presage even the Antichrist from the Book of Revelation. Would this be the type of 'hero' to emerge?

Did Elgar therefore embark on this vast project with the subconscious thought that God, if he existed, would guide his pen, lighting the way to both inspiration and faith? Did failure to realise his concept in its entirety serve to demolish that faith? Perhaps not. Throughout his later life Elgar carried in his pocket book an extract from Jean Paul Richter's *Levana*:

> '. . . when in your last hour (think of this) all faculty in the broken spirit shall fade and die into inanity – imagination, thought, effort, enjoyment – then at last will the night flower of Belief alone continue blooming, and refresh with its perfumes in the last darkness.'[12]

Elgar's attitudes remained mystical. The path he took has been followed by many who find in his work the source of a deep spiritual satisfaction. If one can say anything at all about Elgar's faith it is, surely, that he came to know a personal God – but a God unfettered by any orthodoxy.

CHAPTER TWO

PLOTTING GIGANTIC WORX

Elgar, in later years, explained the concept of the Apostles trilogy as follows: '. . . the idea of the work originated in this way. Mr Reeve [Elgar's schoolmaster] addressing his pupils, once remarked: "The Apostles were poor men, young men, at the time of their calling: perhaps before the descent of the Holy Ghost no cleverer than some of you here." This set me thinking, and the oratorio of 1903 is the result . . . I have been thinking about it since boyhood, and have been selecting the words for years, many years.'[3]

In gratitude for the inspiration of Francis Reeve, Elgar sent him a copy of the completed *Apostles* vocal score. Soon after being knighted (1904), he also sent a copy of Canon Gorton's analysis of the libretto with a note saying: 'Some of your boys try to follow out your good advice and training, although I can answer only for one who falls only too far short of your ideal.'[4]

Alfred H. Brewer, Organist of Gloucester Cathedral with Elgar

But there could have been other, more subtle, influences at work as his composing experience increased. For instance, Elgar's orchestration of Brewer's *Emmaus* for the 1901 Three Choirs Festival is thought to have been highly influential in the decision to embark upon the trilogy.

In 1898 Alfred Herbert Brewer, the newly appointed Organist and Master of the Choristers at Gloucester Cathedral, then aged 33, directed his first Three Choirs Festival. The *Musical Times* noted the appointment, and Elgar – at 41 still a year away from his coming *Enigma* triumph – observed, somewhat waspishly, to August Jaeger that: 'Brewer is very lucky – or rich – to get into the MT before he's done ANYTHING.'[5] Despite this, Brewer had included the 'Meditation' from *The Light of Life* in the 1898 festival. Elgar indicated his annoyance at this in the same letter to Jaeger: '. . . a 3 choir festival always upsets me – the twaddle of it and mutual admiration.'[6]

Brewer's direction of the festivals at Gloucester quickly distinguished itself by the inclusion of much more new music. In 1901 there were eleven premieres by British composers, six of them commissioned, including a piece from Brewer himself. In his *Memories of Choirs and Cloisters*, he recalled: 'on receiving the invitation from the Stewards to write a work for the festival I consulted my friend Joseph Bennett [a prolific librettist of the time] . . . His reply to my appeal was that he would put on his thinking cap and would do all he could to provide me with a necessary book. I did not have long to wait, for within a few days it arrived. It was on the subject of the Disciples' journey to Emmaus, and "Emmaus" was to be the title of the work . . . I became so interested in the subject that I finished the work within four weeks.'[7]

But there was a major, and unexpected, problem. Bennett had some years earlier supplied the same text to another composer, who only learned of, and objected to, Brewer's setting when it was already with the printers. The librettist, quite unruffled despite threats of legal action, rewrote the text for Brewer. But the reworking of the score that this necessitated delayed work so much – still unscored for orchestra within weeks of the festival – that Brewer considered withdrawing it.

Elgar had already been invited by Brewer to conduct *Cockaigne* at the 1901 Festival, but there was, perhaps, more than an eager note in Elgar's acceptance letter of 14 June: 'Jaeger tells me by this post that you are somehow worried – (the exact nuance I don't quite understand – about getting your work ready) – he said something before we left home and I told him you must not be worried and that if necessary to make things smooth I would orchestrate some for you – that's all – I know it's a cheek to offer but if I can save you a little worry let me do so.'[8]

Brewer gratefully accepted and later recalled: '. . . the proof copy of *Emmaus* was sent to Elgar'.[9] Neither the accompanying letter nor Elgar's comments remain, but Brewer responded, on 25 June: 'I am most grateful to you for offering to do so much of the scoring, but there are two numbers I should certainly like you to do . . . With your great powers you could make so much more of them than I ever could – if you are liking to do this will you say which of the numbers mentioned in your letter you will leave me to do instead.'[10]

Five days later, on 30 June, Elgar informed Brewer that he had orchestrated six of the sections (but oddly not the two which the composer had specifically requested). He commented: '. . . if that's not enough you must let me know. I send on my MS. I hope it pleases you but I feel much at sea as to your wishes and am sadly afraid you will not like my interpretation . . . I have *not* revised any of it I fear, as usual there may be errors . . . the first thing however is to know if it will DO at all for you.'[11]

Brewer was obviously relieved and delighted at the result: 'It looks magnificent and in fact you have made my poor little *Emmaus* sound quite beautiful.'[12] Elgar undertook the rest of the scoring, as his letter of 7 July makes clear: 'I shall hope to despatch by an early post tomorrow the remainder of your score . . . I have taken great pleasure in trying to interpret your thoughts and feelings and

George Johnston
Chairman, Birmingham Festival
Orchestral Sub-Committee

only hope I have not grossly misinterpreted them. Now: *please* accept my work on your score and never think I want any return whatever: keep a kind thought for a fellow sometime – that's all . . . I have enjoyed your themes immensely and they lend themselves to colour famously . . . the end is good (as far as you're concerned) but I think you might have instrumented it better than I could have.'[13]

Before the first performance the *Musical Times* thought the music: 'thoughtful and skilful'[14], to which their reviewing critic added, the following month, that it was 'truly devotional, melodious and simple. There is no straining for effect, no make-believe; it is heart-felt music, true and sincere.'[15].

Elgar, as he was working on the orchestration, wrote to Jaeger: 'I have nearly finished Brewer's *Emmaus* and have taken much joy doing it . . . Some of [it] is really beautiful and it *lends itself* to scoring in a ready and exceptional way. I have *not* made an elaborate score – but I hope it's artistic.'[16]

It was while Elgar's mind was engaged on the orchestration that his attention became more focused on his own ideas for the Apostles trilogy, of which the encounter on the road to Emmaus formed part. There are definite echoes of his orchestration work for Brewer in many parts of *The Apostles.*

So it is clear that Elgar thought about the Apostles story on and off for many years and wanted to attempt setting it when offered a commission for a large-scale choral work to be premiered at the Birmingham Triennial Festival in 1900. At that point he was only toying with Cardinal Newman's poem *The Dream of Gerontius* for a work at a later date. All his initial sketches were for a character with whom Elgar found a ready identity – Judas. An unusual choice perhaps, but as an outsider, like Elgar himself, the attraction was magnetic. Judas haunted Elgar for the whole of his creative life, as he haunts the scores of *The Apostles* and *The Kingdom* long after his death.

As ideas for the Apostles project grew in his mind, Elgar realised that he was unequal to the task of shaping an adequate libretto. This would clearly require not only a non-Catholic but also an expert theologian. When he consulted Edward Capel-Cure, who had been his librettist for *The Light of Life,* one problem above all others became clear – there was no time to do the project justice given the ten months remaining before the Birmingham Festival. He had left it too late and determined to give up the commission altogether.

It was the persuasiveness of George Johnstone, Chairman of the Birmingham Festival Orchestral Sub-Committee, which encouraged him to carry on, but only with *The Dream of Gerontius* given the shortage of time. The text, although needing to be severely abridged, was complete. All Elgar had to do was spend a day or two with a priest at the Birmingham Oratory, appropriately editing the poem, and he had a structure around which to compose the music. Despite Elgar's own uncertainty about this he agreed.

Judas plagued him still and he complained to August Jaeger: 'Judas is dropped! . . . I am sick of the whole thing & wd never hear, see, write or think of music in shape, form substance or wraith again.'[17] The Judas sketches did have a use, though. As Elgar told Jaeger: 'I say, that Judas theme will have to be used up for death and despair in this work.'[18] They eventually found their way into

Elgar's original 'Judas' theme

the scene for the Angel of the Agony in *The Dream of Gerontius*. The obvious desolation could, in the end, have fitted either scene.

In reality, and despite the practical reasons for not proceeding with the Apostles project, he had left the composition of *The Dream of Gerontius* almost too late as well: certainly too late for proper rehearsal which, together with other factors beyond Elgar's control, made the failure of the work at its premiere almost inevitable.

The project had been something of a risk, both from Elgar's and the Birmingham Festival Committee's perspective, due to reservations about the subject of Cardinal Newman's poem Dvorak had been dissuaded from using it for the 1888 Festival on religious grounds. But an adaptation could be made comparatively quickly. This was at best a compromise but one that was necessary given the shortage of time remaining. By mid-March 1900 composition was underway and Part One was completed in two months. Part Two took a further two months but the whole process was slowed down by the need to correct the proofs sent from the publishers. It was not until early August 1900 that the orchestration was completed. With the premiere of such an original and complex work only two months away no full orchestral score was available to Hans Richter, the Festival's conductor, until 23 September – only 10 days before he was to conduct it.

Other dimensions of an impending disaster had already occurred. Because of Elgar's slow progress on writing the work, Novello (the music publisher) deferred any work towards producing *The Dream of Gerontius* until they had printed all the music for the September 1900 Three Choirs Festival at Hereford. This, together with Elgar's continued prevarications over altering unacceptable parts of the work, put back the availability of the vocal score for the chorus until early August when they were taking their traditional summer break – rehearsals of *The Dream of Gerontius* were originally scheduled to start in May together with nine major works needing preparation by the chorus (including several other new commissions by British composers). But, perhaps more fatefully for Elgar's work, the chorus-master – Swinnerton Heap, who was to have guided the Festival Chorus through *The Dream of Gerontius,* died suddenly of pneumonia at the age of 53 on 11 June. This experienced musician, who had an enthusiasm for Elgar's music, may have been invaluable given the shortage of time remaining until the premiere. However, although Heap had been a close friend of

Elgar – he was the dedicatee of the Organ Sonata (1895) and *The Light of Life* (1896) – there is evidence that Elgar may have had doubts about his ability to prepare the Birmingham choir, possibly due to declining health. In an unpublished letter to Granville Bantock, Elgar encouraged him to think seriously about applying for the Principal's position at the Birmingham and Midland Institute, and indicated some of the other musical opportunities:

'. . . they don't like Heap as trainer of the Festl. Chorus – you wd. have that & some of the societies round about wd. naturally engage you to conduct: then the Festival wd. sooner or later want a new conductor . . . poor Heap seems to be failing & they have no man worth his salt in B'ham & it can only be a question of a season or two. I don't think he will coach the Chorus for the Festival this year.'[19]

Elgar's attitude towards Heap may also have been coloured by an altercation between the two men at the premiere of *King Olaf* in 1896. Swinnerton Heap had prepared the chorus meticulously for the performance at the North Staffordshire Triennial Festival. But the composer's stress over the work was irrationally turned on a hapless chorus-master in a very public falling out. This became the gossip of the Potteries and completely overshadowed the success of the new work. According to a close friend, 'the breach was never healed.'[20]

As it was the Birmingham Festival authorities pulled his 70 year-old predecessor out of retirement. Quite apart from his potential anti-Catholic views, the replacement chorus-master had neither the energy nor the insight to lead a large group of amateur singers through the complexities of *The Dream of Gerontius*. Chorus rehearsals started again on 20 August. Elgar's work was allotted seven sessions, some of which were shortened because the chorus-master was in failing health. The only combined rehearsal of all participants took place in Birmingham on 29 September. Predictably there were problems that, to the consternation of chorus and orchestra, produced at one point a flaming outburst from Elgar who, unable to contain himself any longer, had left his seat in the hall, mounted the stage and stopped the rehearsal. With hindsight this was, of course, not only a mistake on Elgar's part – he had after all created the situation himself – but it also set up a lingering resentment towards the composer in the whole performing group that may have found its ultimate expression in the shambles of the first performance. This hostility was increased by Hans Richter who, sensing an impossible situation, cut short the rehearsal and closeted himself over the weekend with the score before calling an extraordinary chorus rehearsal on the Monday – the chorus's traditional rest day before the start of the festival. Predictably, after six hours of unscheduled rehearsal, the chorus was thoroughly stale. Parry, whose *De profundis* was premiered the day before Elgar's *Dream of Gerontius*, records how his own work came to grief because the chorus was 'tired out' and 'flabby'. This seems a fair indicator of the problems with the whole festival – a lack of incisive singing from the choir, who seem, literally, to have been overwhelmed. Their lacklustre performance at *The Dream of Gerontius* premiere perhaps said it all – even the conductor refused to acknowledge the chorus's applause for him.

Yet the audience recognised a great work when they heard one and applauded despite this being strictly against festival rules governing morning performances. The music critics were also unanimous in their praise of the music but roundly condemned the performance. Perhaps the fiasco of the premiere effectively delayed many planned British performances because the difficulties presented by Elgar's choral writing were presumed insurmountable.

Ivor Atkins
Organist of Worcester Cathedral

To Elgar the failure seemed complete. He wrote to Jaeger: 'I have worked hard for forty years & at the last, Providence denies me a decent hearing of my work: so I submit – I always said God was against art & I still believe it, anything obscene or trivial is blessed in this world & has a reward . . . I have allowed my heart to open once – it is now shut against every religious feeling & every soft, gentle impulse for ever.'[21] Yet, of course, to some extent Elgar only had himself to blame, but it was to be a lesson from which he did not learn.

When approached by the Birmingham authorities in October 1901 with a commission for the next Festival, some two years away, Elgar returned to the Apostles subject and the offer was accepted. Despite the initial failure of *The Dream of Gerontius*, its subsequent success, first in Germany and gradually in England, had at the age of 44 achieved for him national recognition. The Birmingham Festival authorities were keen to capitalise on this.

Two years seemed enough time for completion of the project, but throughout the first half of 1902 there were many distractions. Other compositions and an increasing number of conducting engagements got in the way. By the end of June that year, however, he seemed ready to begin although eye trouble, which had been a recurring problem, hindered his efforts.

In a letter to Ivor Atkins he wrote: 'I am now plotting GIGANTIC WORX [sic].'[22] Just how gigantic they were to be began to unfold in his mind as at Bayreuth he heard Wagner's *Der fliegende Holländer*, *Parsifal* and, perhaps most notably, the first three operas of the Ring cycle.

In the first diary entry from Alice Elgar, the composer's wife, regarding work on the oratorio she notes that Elgar had begun 'to be very busy collecting material.'[23] In his own accounts of these early considerations Elgar said he studied 'everything I can lay my hands on which bears on the subject directly or indirectly, meditating on all that I have sifted out as likely to serve my purpose.'[24] In March 1903 he gave an interview to Frederick Edwards, a Malvern journalist, in which he told him: 'I have been reading no end of books on divinity for more than a year . . . in order to get thoroughly in touch with my all-absorbing subject.'[25] Whether this was actually the case, given the problems he later experienced in producing the libretto, is open to question.

Elgar's original idea for the overall scheme

Elgar was well aware of his limitations both as librettist and theological scholar, but his suggestion that there was a clear starting-point for the construction of the text after his research is misleading. From correspondence, diary notes and the information which has become available over the years since Elgar's death it is possible to say, with some certainty, that his effort to 'saturate his mind with Biblical literature' was mainly undertaken simultaneously with work on the libretto. This meant that instead of having a fixed base from which to work, the composer was constantly taking on new ideas as his research progressed: a working method which began to put at risk any hope of a coherent oratorio within the rapidly dwindling available time.

Before October 1902, when Elgar obtained a typewriter for work on *The Apostles* libretto, Alice Elgar wrote out all the manuscript text. It seems improbable that Elgar would himself have looked up suitable texts only to dictate them to his wife. It also seems highly unlikely that his wife would have selected the texts on her own. A possible explanation is that he chose the relevant sections from his sources — Bible concordances, etc. — and then asked Alice Elgar to transcribe the actual verses from the Bible, thus giving him access to a copious amount of written material from which to choose.

On his return to England from Bayreuth Elgar penned a brief note of his ideas for the trilogy as he then saw it. The eventual result, however, bore no more than a passing resemblance to this initial scheme, where the three projected oratorios were to be considered simultaneously.

Whether it was the sheer size of the story Elgar set out to tell – an attempt to set virtually the whole New Testament to music – or that it was literally a story without end, he soon realised that this could not be achieved in one work. The concept of Apostleship in the Christian tradition is infinite, and the sweep of this story could find its way into many oratorios on a continuing theme. He had before him the memory of Wagner's Ring heard, in part, earlier that year. So the idea of at least a trilogy of oratorios quickly developed. But whatever was in his mind he had no text or even a plot worked out at that stage, although he promised to have something for either the Birmingham authorities or Novello, who were negotiating with the festival to publish the work, by the autumn.

If Wagner was providing Elgar with inspiration for his project, it is perhaps fair to ask why, when work eventually started, he had still produced little on which to base his music. Wagner would surely never have begun anything without a detailed plot and libretto from which to work. His use of *leitmotif* – the system of creating representational themes for a character, natural element or abstract idea – to cross reference the operas of the Ring would not have been so successful without a completed framework on which to build the music. Elgar, attempting to use a similar system of *leitmotif*, was creating text in response to abstract musical ideas – some set down years earlier – and hoping the whole would grow as if by some divine inspiration. But time was always against composing in such an ill-defined way. Interestingly though, and despite the agonies it produced in his life, this method of haphazard working was echoed in some later advice Elgar gave to his friend Ivor Atkins, who was composing a work for the 1908 Three Choirs Festival but had no suitable text: 'set to work on your new thing at once. Don't wait for words.' [26]

CHAPTER THREE

TO ASSAIL THE CASTLES OF 'THE RING'

Musical ideas always came first for Elgar, with the text and drama being used to develop this. There is no comparison here with Wagner, although Elgar remained preoccupied with Wagner's genius, especially his use of the orchestra, to the end of his life. Wagner's *leitmotifs* were almost always much shorter than Elgar's, which made them easier to combine and aid the musical development of the whole. In the *Ring* cycle Wagner uses only 68 themes, whereas Elgar's 169 identifiable themes (32 of which are shared by *The Apostles* and *The Kingdom*) means that he is using one of these recognisable motifs on average every 5 bars throughout the two completed oratorios of the Apostles trilogy. Perhaps, almost unbelievably, this 'cut and paste' method works 99% of the time, but there are moments when the joins show. A striking example of this is in the orchestral introduction to Part Two of *The Apostles,* where some of the most important themes of the work seem butt-ended together like a line of mismatched bricks.

Elgar had worked with librettos of varying quality for most of his creative life up to that point. He was, at heart, a symphonist but spent a great deal of time in his earlier years writing choral music for the great festivals. Composing to a text solved many of the structural problems that inevitably face composers setting out to write symphonies of four abstract movements. In that case the composer has all the horizontal and vertical problems of structure and form to solve simultaneously.

The Biblical epic of the Apostles story gave him the opportunity, with appropriate help, to create his own libretto without having to rely on something already written. Besides, against the Bible, nothing existed which remotely matched his vision. Using the Bible could also solve another problem. *The Dream of Gerontius* had run into doctrinal trouble with the Anglican authorities because of its overtly Catholic connections, but a New Testament-based text could cause no such offence.

Time had, however, moved on and with less than a year to the premiere of *The Apostles* (Part One) there was no text and only the very roughest outline of the whole trilogy as supplied to the publisher:

I   the schooling [of the Apostles]
II   the earthly result
III   the result of it all in the next world . . . Last Judgement & the next world as in Revelations: each work to be complete in itself – the one bearing on the other[27]

It is not clear how much Elgar had really studied the problem of the text before replying to Birmingham with a plan. What was eventually supplied seems to have been based on Rev. W. H. Pinnock's *Analysis of New Testament History* alone. The layout of the proposed scheme raises an important question, because it may show that initially Elgar planned *The Apostles* as a single work. There is an argument, despite Elgar's own later statements, that the trilogy idea was a face-saving device when he realised that work on *The Apostles* (as originally conceived) could not be completed in time for Birmingham. Evidence for this is said to lie in the fact that the idea of the trilogy is not raised in any correspondence between Elgar and Novello or the Birmingham Festival authorities before November 1902. Also, when Elgar wrote a note to be published with the score (but withdrawn before final printing) he only made reference to two oratorios:

> 'It has long been my wish to compose an oratorio which should embody the Calling of the Apostles, their teaching (schooling) and their Mission, culminating in the establishment of the Church among the Gentiles . . . The present work carries out the first portion of this scheme; <u>the second remains for production on some future occasion.</u>'[28]

Then again, in a letter to Novello nine days after the first performance of *The Apostles*, Elgar indicates that:

> 'I have been thinking earnestly over *The Apostles* & have now definitely decided that the present work must stand alone leaving the continuation of the scheme to be carried out in a <u>work of similar proportions</u> . . . <u>the remainder of the work, in whatever shape it may eventually take, is mine to deal with.</u>'[29]

Nonetheless, the general weight of opinion favours the trilogy theory; a view reinforced by consideration of Elgar's thinking over many years and the knowledge of the inspiration which he found in experiencing the Ring cycle at Bayreuth in 1902.

Finance always played a part in Elgar's thinking and it was the Birmingham Festival authorities' continuing negotiations with the publishers, Novello, which produced the next indication from the composer about the scope of *The Apostles*. He was being pressurised to produce something on which they could base their discussions about payment for the work, and while there was still no sign of any libretto he indicated that:

> the work will be as difficult as Gerontius – except the Demon's Chorus . . . the Chorus work is difficult in the same mystic sort of way as the other work.
> It will take, roughly, two hours.
> It falls naturally into two parts.
> I   The Calling of the Apostles to the Ascension.
> II   The spread of the Gospel until the climax at Antioch.
> ? The soloists are Peter – Baritone
> John – Tenor
> Judas – Bass
> Sopran [sic] – Mary
> Contralto Mary Magdalene & for recits & reflectual [sic] passages[30]

Realising that he could delay decisions no longer, and working against his preferred method of allowing the text to evolve from the music, he put together sufficient material for the libretto of his proposed first section (The Calling of the Apostles to the Ascension) and sent it to Novello. His friend Jaeger was, as always, enthusiastic and encouraging: 'You have set yourself no small task! Some of the "Situations" should give you superb chances for inspired music.'[31] This was in sharp contrast to Novello's management, who now began to see through the delays of the previous six months. There was, in reality, little of any substance that would point to the finished work. Alfred Littleton, Novello's Chairman, remarked in a letter to the Birmingham Festival authorities: 'I could really gather little or nothing from the libretto as it was in such a fragmentary state.'[32] But whatever anxieties Novello might have had, they soon agreed the terms requested. This may have been more to do with a rival bid from another publisher (Boosey) than because of their faith that a finished product could be delivered on time.

Elgar began work on composing *The Apostles* in mid-December 1902 with barely ten months to go before the premiere. By mid-January he had sent off the first two sections – the Prologue and The Calling of the Apostles – to the printers. Encouraged by the supply of the first two scenes, Novello assumed that the full version of the whole libretto was available. The publishers felt that as *The Dream of Gerontius* had made such an impact in Germany, then the new oratorio might also prove popular. Unlike *The Dream of Gerontius,* however, Novello did not want the expense of printing a separate German edition because the translation could be set underneath the English in one edition. As it later turned out, the score of *The Kingdom* was the first to be published with a simultaneous translation.

Realising that he would be unable to produce the libretto in time on his own, Elgar once again sought the help of Edward Capel-Cure. Together they found enough ideas that enabled a more detailed libretto for all the projected scenes in the first part (up to the Ascension) to be supplied. But the scale of the task before him was creating the sort of inspirational paralysis that was to become even more typical as the project progressed.

CHAPTER FOUR

IN LONGDON MARSH

The score of *The Apostles* bears the inscription 'In Longdon Marsh 1902-1903'. Longdon Marsh is a lonely, unbecoming place under the Malvern Hills near Birtsmorton. An old Roman Road runs through it and, apart from this, there appears nothing of the hand of man. Elgar had found it while cycling and would often return there to gain inspiration. For a creative genius, ill at ease with the society in which he was bound to live, it provided the perfect place of escape. He told his friend Billy Reed that the great climaxes in the Ascension sequence of *The Apostles* were planned in that wilderness. The Marsh is surely a metaphor for introspection in Elgar's life.

Much more thinking and agonising was done both there and in the porch of the nearby church at Queenhill. The beautiful little rural church stood then in an isolated spot; today it overlooks the bustle of a busy motorway.

Did Elgar see in this church the symbolic evidence that the mission of the Apostles was miraculously successful through the establishment of the Christian Church? In the early stages, before panic and despair over the project set in, he noted many times in his diary: 'saw Heron fishing'.[33] As time progressed his need for the Marsh became greater: '. . . the weather is too cold for me to go and sit in the Marsh with my beloved wild creatures to <u>get heartened up and general inspiration.</u>'[34] Towards the end of the nightmare over writing *The Apostles* he wrote of the Marsh again, this time to Clare Stuart-Wortley, the daughter of friends, with whose mother he was said to have been deeply in love: '. . . my friend the heron — who stands fishing on one leg . . . we are the only two people who know much about the lonely Marsh & we both love it — he catches frogs & I don't; that's all!'[35]

But inspiration was somehow lacking as he surveyed the disparate sketches and unconnected scenes already composed. Poor health also bothered him and he wrote to Jaeger early in 1903: '. . . lumbago better, rheumatism bad, temper evil, disposition venomous, mind — vacant.'[36] He urged Novello to send the printed proofs of the first two parts to spur him into further action as he set the next section of *The Apostles* — 'By the Wayside', in which

Queenhill Church

Christ speaks the Beatitudes and the different characters in Elgar's version of the Apostles story make their private observations on what is being said. It is here that we encounter Judas for the second time, but once again in a more conventional portrayal of dissidence from the rapt concentration of the other Apostles.

Elgar had greater things planned for Judas that more than challenged the accepted view of this man as wholly evil. That would come later, at a time when his despair over progress in completing even the first oratorio of the trilogy reached its height.

Longdon Marsh – Photographed by Elgar

Elgar's sister 'Dot'

By the end of February 1903 the Beatitudes scene was with the printers but Elgar, now a desperate man, needed guidance through the mass of Biblical material that was accumulating in his study. He sought salvation through his favourite poet Longfellow, whose lengthy poem, *The Divine Tragedy*, offered a useful structure for Elgar's confused thoughts. There was, however, a high price to pay.

Conversion was central to the Apostles story, and, while there were many New Testament examples from which to choose, Longfellow's poem contained only one – that of Mary Magdalene. She was not even a disciple, let alone an Apostle, and her place in Elgar's original scheme was not major. But time was short and she made an instant appeal to Elgar. This was an almost disastrous mistake given the shortage of time before the premiere. It could, of course, be argued that Elgar did not fully understand the process of conversion. His experience was through his mother, his wife and his sister Dot, who wanted to become a nun. Perhaps the freshest memory

16

was, however, of Kundry in Wagner's *Parsifal*, heard at Bayreuth in November 1902. Kundry, a sorceress, who tries to seduce Parsifal in Wagner's opera, has parallels with Mary Magdalene that are not hard to find. She is criticised for attempting a good deed as an atonement for past sins; she appeals for the salvation of Parsifal's redemptive powers as her blasphemous mockery of Christ has led her to wander the world for centuries; she begs to serve the spiritual master Parsifal; finally she bathes Parsifal's feet, then anoints them before drying them with her hair.

Longfellow had enlarged his account of Mary Magdalene's conversion by adding Peter's attempt to reach Christ by walking on water. The number of scenes therefore began to grow in Elgar's mind as he responded to the poem, although not setting any of the actual text. As Mary's conversion and

'Christ in the wilderness'

her seeking salvation, now so central to the message of the oratorio, was dependent upon the earthly Christ, he also had to take on a larger role. Her conversion was clearly not connected with the original Apostles story and the scene was getting out of hand, slowing down not only the story but also work on composing the rest of the oratorio. The whole episode was demanding sacrifices from a concept which was originally intended to show, through the oratorio's main characters, a move from darkness (Judas) to light (the strength of Peter) in the early Church. Elgar's lack of understanding, so far as conversion was concerned, took the main message no further. He failed to

17

show adequately even this one example of conversion, maintaining Mary Magdalene's sorrow right to the end of her long scene. There was no joy at repentance and no time left to modify anything. It was almost the end of March and he had not even completed the first part of the scheme submitted to the Birmingham Festival authorities. If he continued with his proposals, the length of the finished work would be alarming.

From this fraught period an unusual inspiration emerged. Canon Gorton, who had been Elgar's main adviser on Anglican doctrine, invited the composer and his wife to adjudicate at the Morecambe Competitive Music Festival towards the end of April 1903. While the Elgars came away from the Lancashire seaside town very much unimpressed by their experiences, Elgar had seen a reproduction of a painting, *Christ in the Wilderness* (1872), by the Russian artist Ivan Kramskoi. The artist said of the picture: '. . . this is no Christ, it is the image of the sorrows of humanity which are known to us all.'[37] But for Elgar it became his 'ideal picture of the Lonely Christ'[38] that he was seeking to enshrine in his music for *The Apostles*. He obtained a copy of the picture and hung it on his study wall, where it remained for years afterwards.

CHAPTER FIVE

THE DARK NIGHT OF THE SOUL

However far work on *The Apostles* was falling behind, and whatever stress this was causing him, Elgar was unable to spend all of his time on composing. He was much in demand nationally as a conductor of his own works. It was, therefore, not until April 1903 – only six months from the premiere – that he began more consistent work on the score. But this time he was on safer ground with a character he fully understood and with whom he sympathised – Judas.

Despite Elgar's rather more conventional portrayal of Judas in the earlier scenes of *The Apostles*, he eventually portrayed him not as a self-seeking villain but as an intellectual, an outsider who believed in Christ but doubted whether He would manifest Himself. Judas was not prepared to wait; he attempted to force Christ's hand by putting Him in a position where He would have to do something miraculous. Then the people would believe in Him as Judas did himself. He wanted to be assured, to have his certainty backed up by the certainty of others. When he saw that his gamble has failed, suicide was the only way out. It is now believed that as Elgar wrote the inspired scenes for Judas, his despair over *The Apostles*, his lack of faith (both in the conventional sense and in himself) together with personal problems, possibly including guilt over his love for Alice Stuart-Wortley, led him to contemplate a similar end for himself.

He was eventually to say about this episode: . . . 'to my mind Judas'

Alice Stuart-Wortley
A portrait by her father, Millais

crime & sin was <u>despair</u>, not only at the betrayal which was done for worldly purposes. In these days, when every "modern" person seems to think that "suicide" is the actual way out of everything, my plan, if explained, may do some good.'[39] Self-doubt was a characteristic of Judas which found a ready echo in a composer now under great stress.

Although Elgar often wrote his oratorio solo passages with particular singers in mind, when work began on the Judas scene no final decision had been taken about who would sing the part. He was by this time despairing of finding any English singers who could adequately realise the roles of Judas and Peter. He complained to Jaeger: 'Oh! these [English] singers - *where* are their *brains?*'[40] He really wanted the Dutch singer, Anton van Rooy, for Judas but also tried to get Ludwig Wüllner – the singer who had performed the bass solos in the first triumphant German performance of *The Dream of Gerontius.* Both were noted Wagnerians and would produce the right colour for what he envisaged. Elgar regarded English voices as too 'white' in this respect. He was eventually persuaded against using foreign soloists following a performance of *The Dream of Gerontius* in the newly built Westminster Cathedral when critical reaction pointed to their difficulty with singing English. Andrew Black eventually took the part, even though Elgar originally wanted him for Peter. In the end, who was to sing the role could have made no difference to Elgar's magnificent characterisation of Judas.

Having failed Elgar in 1900 over *The Dream of Gerontius* premiere, the Birmingham chorus was anxious to begin rehearsals for the new work. They had a debt of honour to repay, but this very understandable concern, coming just five months before the first performance of a work which was not even half-written – indeed no libretto had been submitted for the second or third parts of this first oratorio – forced Elgar to revise the scheme, making it, at this stage, a pale reflection of the original proposals. The vision would get paler still as time progressed. In any event, some of the music that was being written reflected Elgar's lack of inspiration and appeared almost meaningless. Still, in June 1903, he promised Novello all the oratorio's remaining parts 'without delay'[41] as preparations for a special performance of *The Dream of Gerontius* in Westminster Cathedral approached.

He returned to the remaining scenes in Part II, but the major events which they portrayed – the Crucifixion and the Resurrection – were passed almost in the blink of an eye as he moved on to the great Ascension scene. Was this an attempt to shift attention away from Christ and back to the Apostles themselves; were these scenes that he could not bring himself to set; or was he simply short of time and, in any event, considering with alarm the growing scale of this single oratorio?

After conducting what turned out to be a triumphant performance of *The Dream of Gerontius* in the almost completed Westminster Cathedral, Elgar returned to Malvern sick with worry. Longdon Marsh drew him back again and again as he shaped the climaxes of the Ascension. The solitude and the desolation of the place somehow helped him with a choral ensemble that he was never to equal. But it was not the end for Part II that he had originally envisaged, and revisions to the earlier parts of the work – some already printed – were now needed.

In July, with the 'Ascension' scene almost complete, Elgar travelled to London for the first performance of the *Coronation Ode,* postponed from 1902 when the King's sudden illness had forced the cancellation of the planned Coronation. Despite the major triumph of this work at its premiere, preoccupation with the incomplete Apostles was a continuing nightmare. When Elgar arrived back in Malvern he found an anxious letter from August Jaeger waiting for him:

August Jaeger

My dear E.

Here are some more proofs.
May I make a polite suggestion? Time is flitting fast & we should have got Part I of the *Apostles* to B'ham long ago. But the corrections are so fearful & so upsetting . . . that I get heart broken over the delays & worries. Whatever you do — although as you know, we are most anxious to do all you wish — don't make any more alterations just now than are absolutely imperative, the expense is a detail — it is the delay which I deplore so greatly . . . at present it seems to me fatal to the proper rehearsing of the work. Don't be cross with me; I write only to save, if possible, a repetition of the 1900 collapse, due to want of sufficient rehearsing.'[42]

It was at this point, less than four months before the premiere and when the work should have been well into rehearsal, that Elgar had to accept the reality of the situation. Unless the score was finished without delay he faced another disaster on the scale of the *Gerontius* failure. He could not take the risk and retreated, deciding that the oratorio must end with the Ascension. But what real excuses could be offered after so much had been promised? Novello were told by Elgar that: 'I have been seeing my London doctor & my eyes are again in trouble — he forbids more work.'[43] They suggested a postponement but Elgar would not agree. The Birmingham Festival authorities clearly took alarm at the real reasons for curtailment becoming public knowledge. George Johnstone indicated to Elgar that: 'It is well that the public should simply understand that the work is *practically* a complete one, and no mention should be made of the fact that the third part was originally intended to be written. I think this is absolutely necessary for your own sake as well as for the Festival.'[44] With the publishers the festival authorities were more direct, acknowledging that

Part of an unused 'Apostles' scene

Part III had actually been abandoned but rationalised this by suggesting that its inclusion would have unacceptably lengthened the work and might have seemed an anti-climax after the Ascension scene.

Material that Elgar had already composed as part of his original scheme was lost by this and other major modifications during composition of both *The Apostles* and *The Kingdom*. These scenes were more than merely sketches. In some cases they were fully worked but could not be fitted into the subsequent shape of either work. Two of these, for *The Apostles,* should be mentioned. It was Elgar's original intention to set a 'solitary prayer' for Christ near the start of the oratorio. Libretto notes quote Latham's *Pastor pastorum* reference: 'Solitary prayer on our Lord's part commonly betokens some important step in His course of proceeding.'[45] He compiled an appropriate text, fully working the sketch showing the idea of Christ and a rural scene. The Gregorian Gradual *Constitues eos,* which Elgar had relied on for much of *The Apostles* thematic material, is described as 'getting stronger.'[46] Elgar concluded the collection of *leitmotif* settings by writing "this is sufficient material . . . also combination of Apostles & Gospel"[47] which indicated the final shape of the whole in his thinking. Later he added a sequence that in the actual oratorio is set to another text and sung by the Angel.

The second major omission comes from Section Two, 'By the Wayside'. This scene was altered many times around the central idea of the Beatitudes. Elgar wrote in the libretto notes a quotation from Hillard's *A Continuous Narrative of the Life of Christ in the Four Gospels,* 'the revolution Christ is going to cause in men's ideas of goodness.'[48] The small scene was originally continued using Peter's words from Matthew 14: 'Behold, we have forsaken all, and followed thee; what shall we have therefore?' This verse is marked in Elgar's *Red Letter New Testament*[49] and his *Liverpool Bible*[50] and then taken forward in the story of the young man who went away sorrowful at his own inability to renounce his riches. The text, almost inevitably, involved a predictable remark from Judas: 'For he hath great possessions'. The music was written and includes, in the Judas comment, the same thematic idea from the Beatitudes that describes his death in the finished oratorio. It is clear that Elgar initially felt extremely satisfied with the whole scene and even gave it page numbers for the vocal score. Its abandonment was on the grounds of length and not inspiration.

Basic composition of *The Apostles* was effectively completed by the end of June 1903, less than four months before the first performance. Whatever the reasons given for the form in which it was eventually produced, the failure to achieve his vision was already weighing heavily on Elgar and there was much yet left to do. The scoring alone was a daunting prospect.

CHAPTER SIX

RELEGATING AN INFINITY OF THINGS TO THE SHADOWY MORROW

Elgar began scoring *The Apostles* on 29 June 1903 and completed much of Part I during a holiday near Betws-y-Coed, North Wales, in July. This was a relaxed time after all the recent struggles. The orchestration was a continuing triumph and did much to divert him from the feelings of failure about leaving the oratorio in an unfinished state. Of course, he now had a structure on which to work rather than the desolation of empty pages. He returned to Malvern and completed the orchestration on 17 August.

The full score bears an inscription quoted from William Morris's *Earthly Paradise*:

> To what a heaven and earth might grow
> If fear beneath the earth were laid,
> If <u>hope</u> failed not nor <u>love</u> decayed.

It is interesting that autograph scores of Elgar's three largest religious choral works bear inscriptions that at first sight may appear entirely in context. He chose Ruskin for *The Dream of Gerontius,* but the choice of William Morris, a socialist who in Morris's own words was 'careless of metaphysics and religion',[51] perhaps needs some consideration. Although eventually a follower of parliamentary Fabianism, he was quoted as saying, in 1895: 'I do declare that any other state of society than communism is grievous and disgraceful to all who belong to it.'[52] His participation in public demonstrations had twice led to his arrest. Morris's use of the word 'communism' was not in the accepted modern sense and he employed paid labourers in his own factory. He was more of an early democrat who never reconciled ideal socialism with the necessities of production via capitalism.

Was Elgar really familiar with Morris's views or did he simply respond to the poetic works? Was the composer trying to indicate, in a subtle way, by quoting Morris (and previously Ruskin), that their overt criticism of Victorian society's values was really to his taste? While Elgar used a Morris quotation again in 1905 when he said: 'and so I, the idle singer of an empty day, became a Professor of Music',[53] overall the choice of Morris seems an odd one for the introduction to a religious choral work.

The quotation is taken from the last three lines of Apollo's song in *The Love of Alcestis*. This pagan song epitomises Morris's view of an earthly paradise where the god Apollo, who has been exiled from heaven (for slaying the Cyclops), has become a shepherd-musician and takes a different view of the world to that which he formerly held. The first verse is addressed to the human race, urging them to be content in the beautiful world in which they live, as the Gods have abandoned them. In the second verse Apollo entreats Zeus to come down and participate in the perfect earthly paradise.

Anyone seeing the Morris inscription on the score of a religious oratorio, and without knowing the context from which it came, would, not unnaturally, accept it as referring to the Christian state of paradise. The author, of course, never intended this but Elgar may have found the poem attractive at a time of stress following the first failed performance of *The Dream of Gerontius*. His faith, not only spiritual but in the future generally, was being severely tested. It is perhaps easy to see that the failure of love and faith in his own life would lead him towards another view entirely. The underlining of the words 'hope' and 'love' were Elgar's own but in this context the use of the word 'love' is the more Christian one which he again referred to when writing to Walford Davies in 1908, after a performance of the First Symphony: '. . . there is no programme beyond a wide experience of human life with a great charity (love) and a *massive* hope in the future.'[54]

Whatever words of hope he used to preface the score of the *Apostles* could not mask the feelings of failure that preoccupied him. There was, however, a public image to maintain and damage limitation may have been in his mind when he was interviewed by R. J. Buckley, a Birmingham journalist, for an article, 'Dr Elgar at Home'. He insisted that: 'I have been thinking about it [the Apostles subject] since boyhood and have been selecting the words for years, many years. I am my own librettist; some day I will give you my ideas on the relationship between librettist and composer.'[55] But where had these words been when he actually needed them?

With *The Dream of Gerontius* failure at the 1900 festival still in his mind, Elgar determined to conduct the premiere of *The Apostles* himself. This time everything went according to plan, from rehearsals to the performance itself, and on 14 October 1903 Birmingham Town Hall was filled to capacity, with extra seats being brought in. Clearly the festival was centred on this performance and the press was there in force. Reactions were, predictably, somewhat mixed but on the whole enthusiastic. Some of the more perceptive critics withheld their overall conclusions and concentrated on the work's obviously unfinished state. Despite a vigorous defence by Elgar's friends and admirers the critics remained unconvinced. They were waiting for the continuation before passing final judgment. For three at least, the confusion was manifest:

'it presents rather a series of more or less detached pictures or scenes which are ultimately to lead to a definite end.'[56]

'its shifting pictures convey an impression of illusiveness. The central idea is not clear . . . as a whole his [Elgar's] specific musical invention has not been equal to his imagination . . . But I must admit that it is apt to be illuminative on paper more than in hearing unless the invention of themes is distinctive. They must have an unmistakable character . . . or else they conjure up no definite ideas, and their constant recurrence either passes unnoticed in the swirl of the orchestral current, or it seems to produce a feeling of irritation; one has a feeling of chasing shadows.'[57]

'It may be true that the method here so conspicuously exemplified helps the composer in the accomplishment of his work by reducing it to a level of a mere deftness, but it is possible to buy ease as well as gold at too high a price.'[58]

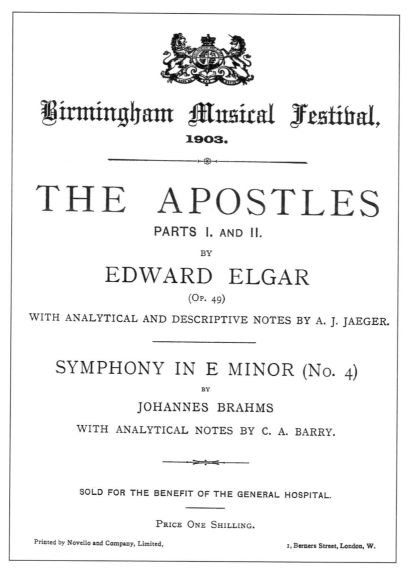

Jaeger's 'Apostles' analysis
Sold at the first performance

The public's reaction was more difficult to gauge as the immediate impact that *The Apostles* made was generally felt to be less than that of *The Dream of Gerontius*. Perhaps they did not understand what Elgar was trying to say. This was despite the fact that the programme – priced one shilling –

contained all the text plus the 'Analytical and Descriptive Notes' by A. J. Jaeger. It is, however, possible that all this material confused the audience as Jaeger had insisted on giving titles to many of the musical themes – much, it seems, to the amazement of the composer. Canon Gorton's 'Interpretation' of the libretto was also available for purchase. In the light of all this information it was perhaps wise for Elgar not to proceed with his own notes, which may have outdone both of the others. From the drafts it is clear that he had widely researched many small matters and made appropriate comments. Some examples of these are the background to 'the acceptable year of the Lord'; the derivation of the name Nazareth; identifying the Horns of Hattin as the probable place where both the Apostles were called and the Sermon on the Mount preached; possible reasons for the storms on the Sea of Galilee; the fact that the soldiers with Judas should have been Roman; Jesus's last words from the Cross ('Eli, Eli, lama sabachtani') being not Hebrew but Chaldean.[59] The list was almost endless and leads to the view that Elgar probably researched too widely given the shortage of time.

It is also probably true to say that *The Apostles* was appreciated by the audience at its first performance more out of respect for Elgar as a composer than because of any great enthusiasm for such a complex work. Jaeger had feared as much some months before: '*The Apostles* is certainly your maturest and greatest work; the certainty of touch and style displayed throughout is wonderful . . . But it is all so original, so individual and subjective that it will take the British public ten years to let it soak into its pachydermal mind . . . I believe that by the time you have completed Part III you will have given the world the greatest oratorio since the *Messiah*.'[60] While some of this praise may be seen as encouragement to a composer who knew he had failed, even at that stage, to realise his vast concept, Jaeger's assertion of a ten-year assimilation was to prove optimistic.

Elgar's friend Canon Gorton summed up the thoughts of those who knew what a struggle completion of the oratorio had been. He wrote to Alice Elgar: 'I have come away with the longing for the completion. I hope he will never again run the risk to himself of working against time, but that he will carve out for himself time, and rest to complete the message.'[61] But this was to be a forlorn hope.

On the surface, at least, Elgar appeared satisfied with the overall result, though less so when Novello tried to renegotiate his fee on a two-thirds only basis because the work was incomplete. This haggling, in reality, further deepened Elgar's depression over his failure with *The Apostles*. Focusing his disappointment on the financial returns was a way of diverting himself from feelings of guilt. In addition to the letters which he sent to Novello complaining about their approach, he tried to enlist the support of Lord Northampton, a staunch ally, who had by coincidence recently returned from Bayreuth, where he found Wagner's *Parsifal* 'ennobling & soul stirring – its only rival is *The Apostles*.'[62] He gently chided Elgar over his attitude to money and continued: 'You have moved men's souls to the highest truths of Christianity & then you say <u>in a fit of depression</u> "as ever, unprofitable".'[63]

When the full fee was eventually forthcoming it encouraged Elgar to consider continuing with the project and he indicated this to his publishers:

'My ideas now revert to my colossal scheme of years ago - but I may not live to do it.

I   The Apostles (which you have)
II   A continuation as talked over with you &
III   The Church of God (or Civitas Dei)! ... I have the IIIrd part libretto done in
      one shape'[64]

He *did* have a libretto for the final part but not from *his* Apostles project material. What already existed was a selection of texts arranged by a friend, Minnie Baker, in 1894, for another choral project entirely.

There was no immediate response from Novello and the matter rested at that point. Canon Gorton raised the continuation in a letter to Elgar: 'I have constantly in mind your future development of Apostles. What will you do with S. Paul?'[65] This was one of many approaches which had started with an enquiry from Capel-Cure about the sequel less than two weeks after the premiere of *The Apostles* – 'Pentecost we have already discussed & I know how magnificently you will develop its musical possibilities – but after that, what next?'[66] It was raised again in a magazine article during May 1904, when there appeared to be a definite intention of completing two more oratorios in line with a modified scheme: 'It was part of my original scheme to continue *The Apostles* by a second work carrying on the establishment of the Church among the Gentiles. This, too, is to be followed by a third oratorio, in which the fruit of the whole – that is to say, the end of the world and the Judgment – is to be exemplified.'[67] But, once again, no more work was done towards the project.

Elgar was by now becoming an even more important national musical figure. Whatever private fears he had about being forgotten and his music having no value in the long term, all the public indications were to the contrary. Several honorary degrees were awarded and there was a three-day festival of his music at Covent Garden attended by the King and Queen. All this for a self-taught provincial composer was overwhelming enough, but the greatest single honour was his knighthood, conferred on 5 July 1904.

Whether he thought any more about his promise to continue with the Apostles project in the midst of this is unclear, for it was not until October 1904, after a performance of *The Apostles* at the Three Choirs Festival in Gloucester, that an approach was made by the Birmingham Festival authorities for a continuation. He appeared enthusiastic and immediately indicated to Novello that he was hard at work on the new oratorio, although not able to supply any material. This was, of course, all too reminiscent of what happened in 1902 but his publishers, to whom he was now proving very profitable, seemed prepared once again to take things on trust. Although he indicated to them that he felt under pressure from other commitments, they encouraged him to accept the first Professorship of Music at Birmingham University, little realising the difficulties this would create later when he was, yet again, working against time to complete a major oratorio commission. Also, as his celebrity status grew his personal appearances increased dramatically. Whereas before there had been some solitude to aid his writing, this was now largely denied him.

At last, in February 1905, he realised that work on *The Apostles* (Part Two) must start if another near disaster was to be avoided. A Biblical text, condensing the concept of the Apostles project as a whole, was assembled by Capel-Cure. This was the way things should have originally been done but Elgar, losing interest, showed the words to his friend Ivor Atkins who set them as his own *Hymn of Faith* for the 1905 Three Choirs Festival in Worcester.

If it really was eye trouble that had plagued him while composing *The Apostles,* this had not recurred but he now began to suffer from violent headaches that, on occasions, prevented him from conducting. By July 1905, after returning from an extended tour of America, he had been unwilling (or unable) to write any music since the *Introduction and Allegro for Strings,* finished in mid-February.

Elgar with the score of 'The Kingdom', in his study at Hereford

The academic appointment in Birmingham had somehow disabled him. When Jaeger raised the subject of *The Apostles* (Part Two) due for performance in less than 15 months, Elgar angrily denied all knowledge of the commission saying: 'I know nothing about the Apostles pt.2 . . . life is now one incessant answering of letters & music is fading away.'[68]

During a 1905 Three Choirs Festival performance of *The Apostles* at Worcester, Elgar's imagination was once again stirred, this time by a local baritone who sang the part of Peter. What sketches existed for the Apostles continuation centred on Peter as a heroic figure in the early Church. But nothing more was done and, instead, Elgar chose to accept an invitation to cruise with the British Fleet in the Mediterranean as a guest of the Royal Navy, leaving an anxious Jaeger to ponder over the fate of *The Apostles* continuation due for the Birmingham Festival now just a year away:

> 'Only! – What about *'Apostles Part II'* for B'ham next year!? I begin to fear me we shall hope in vain to see our soaring expectations fulfilled.'[69]

Returning in mid-October, Elgar went to Norwich for a performance of *The Apostles* at the festival. Fritz Kreisler was to perform there and wanted to meet Elgar, who he regarded as 'the greatest living composer'.[70] Kreisler was clearly looking for Elgar to write 'something for the violin'.[71] This put at further risk work on the new oratorio as Elgar immediately began sketching material for a Violin Concerto.

He was now working only fitfully on *The Apostles* (Part Two) in the time between his other commitments. The academic work at Birmingham was weighing him down and his controversial lectures had not generally been well received. These responsibilities, together with an extended concert tour, saw Elgar once again sick with worry over the Birmingham Festival commission. He therefore decided to restrict the new oratorio by effectively adding only the third part of the original scheme proposed in 1902 – taking the action as far as the establishment of the Christian Church at Antioch. Even that was a daunting prospect given the shortage of time, although he had sufficient unused material from *The Apostles* (Part One) on which to work and provide the basic framework. But again there was no libretto, only musical ideas. Each section he worked on became more difficult and there was so little to show by the end of November 1905 that Alice Elgar recorded in her diary: '. . . much worried – Fate of *Apostles* for Festival trembling in the balance.'[72]

Although the Birmingham University Lectures were coming to an end, controversy about them continued unabated. Elgar was too blunt for the conservative musical establishment and, as a non-academic – an outsider like his Judas in *The Apostles* – failed to take them with him. If he had hoped for some respite from the stress-induced illnesses of recent months, it did not come with the ending of the lectures, for when he returned to serious work on *The Apostles* (Part Two) in mid-December, his headaches worsened. He wrestled with the concepts set out in an article, sent in proof form, by the Dean of Westminster (Armitage Robinson), entitled 'History of the Apostolic Age' (eventually destined for inclusion in *The Cambridge Companion to the Bible*). This was intended to help the composer but all that eventually resulted were more detailed notes about the distinction between the formation of the 'Jewish Christian Church' and 'Churches wholly or in part Gentile'.[73] His overall depression was summed up in a letter to the composer Walford Davies at the end of December 1905: 'I am the same depressed (musically) being & the same very much alive (chemically

& every other 'ally') mortal; keen for everything except my avocation [sic], which I feel is not my vocation by a long tract of desert.'[74]

The first pages of the new work were sent to the publishers in early January 1906, together with the suggestion for a title – *The Kingdom of God*. This material was largely choral similar to the Prologue of *The Apostles*. Novello's were not happy with the oratorio's proposed title and Elgar was forced to rethink his whole approach. He decided to replace the Prologue with a large-scale orchestral Prelude, described in a letter to Jaeger (who was by now in a Swiss hospital) as: 'So far . . . the best thing I have done *I know*.'[75] By mid-January this was with the publishers and Elgar seemed in a better frame of mind. There was also the beginning of a major change in his religious outlook. Elgar's faith – never strong – had been severely tested over *The Apostles* and he now began to take on more humanistic concepts that seemed to suit him better. This, though, did not fit too easily with the work he was engaged in. The optimism did not last and within a matter of days, after completing part of the first scene – 'In the Upper Room' – the vision had once again become blurred. Elgar was severely depressed. He turned to finishing a setting of the Lord's Prayer – started three years earlier – as an ending to the first part of the oratorio and then worked steadily at the remaining parts of the first scene. Inspiration came and went, his mood lightened and darkened as he turned again and again to unused *Apostles* material, rewriting it to make the ideas fit into his scheme. With only the Prelude and the first scene completed, with no proper sketches for anything else, and with the prospect of another lengthy American tour in the spring, the task before him looked overwhelming. He now had barely eight months to complete the work. At the end of January 1906, he decided to resign the Birmingham commission.

Alice Elgar

31

Thus Elgar's lifelong fear of failure was about to be realised. Alice Elgar noted in her diary that he was 'less vivacious & more self-assertive in opinion.'[76] One of the scenes he was working on — later discarded — concerned the new Church at Antioch. He noted in the margin of a source book, Page and Walpole's *The Acts of the Apostles,* where the author's note that the term 'Christian' had been used in a contemptuous way initially: 'Contemptuously all the better: contempt is our lot here.'[77] A crisis of faith in himself was clearly engulfing Elgar but it was at that point that his wife took over. Determined that a failure could not be allowed to happen, she devised a scheme with the publishers and the Birmingham Festival authorities that would save not only the project but also Elgar's self-respect. As with *The Apostles* in 1903, the scope of the new oratorio had to be reduced to manageable proportions. Elgar himself doubted whether he could undertake even half the original scheme — now settled as from the reassembly of the Apostles after the Ascension, through the drama of Pentecost, the arrest of Peter and John, their release and then the whole company looking forward to the establishment of the Church finishing with the Lord's Prayer — but reluctantly agreed: 'I wd. prefer *not* to do it but it seems the only way to make things pleasant for everybody & I suppose it must be done.'[78] With the press already asking questions about his state of health it was decided, by all concerned, but particularly the Birmingham Festival authorities, that the failure to complete the oratorio was to be kept strictly secret. It was insisted that the work in its new state represented everyone's understanding of Elgar's plan up to that point.

With the pressure partially lifted, Elgar returned to the score in mid-February, nursed and protected by his wife. Some of the old enthusiasm inspired the music but there were poorer passages as well. Jaeger was less than enthusiastic over some of it but Elgar was oblivious to any criticism as Alice Elgar intercepted letters and kept the harmful ones away. So by the end of March 1906 the oratorio in its new form was more than half-finished, with enough time, even given an extended tour of America during April and May, to complete it.

Work on orchestrating the oratorio began during the American tour and the score bears the inscription 'in Cincinnati, April 1906'. Despite conducting and social engagements Elgar managed to complete the scoring of everything to the end of the first scene. However, his headaches and general feelings of depression continued much as they had done ever since he belatedly started work in earnest the previous winter. By the time he returned to England at the end of May there was little to inspire him and nothing more was composed until almost the end of June, as illness had effectively prevented any activity. During this time it was decided simply to call the new work *The Kingdom* in response to an urgent request from the Birmingham authorities, who wanted to publicise the premiere of the oratorio. Concern was also being expressed by Novello and Co. about their ability to print the music in time for rehearsals, and Elgar was only partially able to reassure them. His mood-swings were still so unpredictable that days went by without anything tangible to show for his efforts.

Yet out of that darkness something did emerge as Elgar completed the longest solo passage in either *The Apostles* or *The Kingdom.* The Virgin Mary's soliloquy 'The Sun Goeth Down' is the heart of Elgar and was started during slightly more optimistic times the previous November. Its text had been painstakingly assembled, its music rivaling anything he had ever written or was to write, and its orchestration a work of sheer genius. Whether the Virgin Mary was ever intended to assume the position which Elgar gives her in this scene of glorious desolation is uncertain but, as with Judas, his identification with her despair is almost unique. Even the inspiration which went to producing that vision of Jesus's triumph through the eyes of his grieving mother was not enough to heal the man who had lost confidence both in himself and his music. Long after Elgar gave up all thoughts of completing the Apostles trilogy, and conducting *The Apostles* and *The Kingdom* had become a chore, it was this passage that never failed to bring tears to the ageing composer's eyes.

The end of Elgar's nightmare was now in sight as he worked on the final scene of the oratorio but, as with *The Apostles,* it was not the ending he had envisaged when he started out. This hushed finale left no real hope for the project's continuation. By 23 July 1906 the work was finished and a week later in Hereford he turned to completing the orchestration, which was to take a month. All was finally with the publishers by the end of August. The score is headed with a quotation from the Canadian poet, Bliss Carman (1861 - 1929):

> I would write
> 'A Music that seems never to have known Dismay, nor haste, nor wrong'

— apt indeed in view of the difficulties which Elgar actually experienced in producing the work at all. Interestingly, he had these words in mind just before the premiere of *The Apostles* and wrote them into his own printed score of that work on 7 October 1903 with the rather telling comment: 'An *Aspiration* E.E.'[79] He pasted into the same score four photographs of his beloved Longdon Marsh from where so much inspiration had come.

The Bliss Carman quotation is perhaps meant to echo the spirit of *The Kingdom* as being more tranquil than that of *The Apostles.* The words come from a poem, 'Daphne', published in *The Pipes of Pan - From the Book of Myths* (London, 1903). The poet was regarded as a gentle mystic, in tune with nature, and the quotation that Elgar uses actually refers to birds singing:

> [Where all day long
> The brown birds make their song —]
> A music that seems never to have known Dismay, nor haste, nor wrong

As with *The Apostles,* Elgar determined to conduct the premiere of *The Kingdom* himself. Rehearsals went well and on the morning of 3 October 1906 the oratorio received its first performance to a packed and expectant festival audience. It had been preceded the night before by *The Apostles.* Elgar always intended that, if possible, the two works should be performed consecutively or as near together as could be achieved. This, of course, was rarely to happen in the future, even at the Three Choirs Festival after they were initially given "side by side" at Gloucester in 1907. Once again, reactions were mixed but on the whole positive with some notable exceptions. Ernest Newman thought that:

'The general level of inspiration is, in my opinion, below that of *Gerontius* or *The Apostles*. Some of the choral portions are so obvious in sentiment that one can hardly believe they came from the delicately spiritual brain that conceived *Gerontius* . . . A good deal of the music must frankly be called dull in itself, but Elgar is now so consummate a master of effect, particularly of orchestral and choral effect, that he can often almost persuade us against our own judgement that the actual tissue of the music is better than it really is.'[80]

Jaeger's 'Kingdom' analysis
Sold at the first performance

Joseph Bennett, the long-serving critic of The Daily Telegraph, who had seen the vocal score before the premiere, commented:

> 'In *The Kingdom,* the kingdom is still to desire, and on almost the last page believers are praying, "Thy Kingdom come".'[81]

The review for *The Daily News* seemed to identify the main problem and hint at the difficulties Elgar had experienced:

> 'The filling of the disciples with the Holy Spirit [in Scene III] is, no doubt, the dramatic, or even theatrical, climax of the oratorio, but the composer's intention has been to deal with the teaching of the Apostles, and therefore the oratorio could not end at what seems a natural conclusion. But having that intention Sir Edward ought surely to have planned his music on different lines.'[82]

Public opinion was, once again, difficult to gauge but, on the whole, probably indifferent. The great scheme on which Elgar had placed so much reliance to take his music forward had ended in nothing but darkness and he would need time to recover. Any idea of another oratorio to continue the theme appalled him. He wanted to compose a symphony but was not yet ready. Writing to Frank Schuster in a fit of depression soon after the first performance he said: 'I don't seem to realise that I have written anything & am trying to forget all about it & myself.'[83] His failure to achieve the vision remained and, following a performance of *The Kingdom* in Cambridge, A. C. Benson (who had provided the text for the *Coronation Ode*) recalled that:

> 'he [Elgar] said simply that it was no sort of pleasure to him to hear *The Kingdom,* because it was so far behind what he had dreamed of – it only caused him shame and sorrow . . . He seemed all strung out on wires, & confessed that he had petitioned for a seat close to the door, that he might rush out if overcome.'[84]

But even at this point there was evidence to suggest that Elgar wanted to do something positive about redressing the balance. In one of his printed vocal scores of *The Kingdom* he had sketched out four extra passages as additions to Scene IV. 'The Sign of Healing', and Scene V. 'The Upper Room'. These items, 'omitted in first edn.', were to be added to the 'existing vocal score . . . from original MS'.[85] They include a chorus of 'peaceful faith' with soloists to be inserted before the contralto solo which opens Scene IV; a solo aria for Peter to follow the previous contralto solo in Section IV; the addition of chorus into John and Peter's duet preceding 'The Arrest' in Scene IV which would have lengthened it considerably. The final insert at the beginning of Scene V was for soloists and chorus but is marked 'practically unaccpd.'.[86] There is no note of Elgar's real intentions and the reference remains obscure.

He continued to conduct performances of *The Apostles* and *The Kingdom* at regular intervals but in early December 1907 Elgar formally told Novello that he had decided not to proceed with the third oratorio of the trilogy. At the same time he started serious work on his First Symphony. It was the year of his 50th birthday.

Echoes of *The Apostles* and *The Kingdom* sound throughout the Symphony and especially 'the inspiration which was carried on the wind, disturbing the grass of Longdon Marsh, was given expression in pure, abstract arts'.[87] It is, perhaps, questionable whether he would have attempted such a work had it not been for the failure of the Apostles project. But the symphony succeeded as an abstract work perhaps because it was not tied to any story. Here was the freedom denied by the confines of a Biblical or any other epic. There were no dissenting voices after the triumphant first performance:

> 'It bears out a contention . . . that Elgar's genius lies in the direction of orchestral music rather than towards choral composition. In the symphony there is a completeness of utterance that we do not find in either *The Apostles* or *The Kingdom*.'[88]

> 'It is quite clear that Elgar has found a new vein . . . the symphony is genuinely new Elgar, new in both feeling, in idiom, and in workmanship.'[89]

But the temptation to complete the trilogy remained, whatever indication Elgar had given to Novello in 1907. He turned back to his sketches in the summer of 1909, the year that should have seen the trilogy completed for Birmingham although, wisely perhaps, no commission had been offered.

He had written no more large-scale religious choral music since completing *The Kingdom*. There had been another symphony and the Violin Concerto. Unable to face anything remotely spiritual, he chose instead to set Arthur O'Shaughnessy's poem 'The Music Makers' as his next major choral work, in 1912. This autobiographical piece used material from many of Elgar's works, but only one reference from *The Apostles*. The failure was still too painful and when Ivor Atkins asked if the third oratorio of the trilogy could be written for the 1914 Three Choirs Festival, Elgar declined on financial grounds.

CHAPTER SEVEN

THE FIELDS ARE AS BARE
AS MY MIND & SOUL

There was to be little large-scale choral music after that. He had probably proved to himself that it was almost impossible to allow his own words to grow with his music in a concurrent evolution. Elgar had adopted this approach willingly in *The Apostles* and it could have worked successfully given more time. Its ultimate failure as a concept now persuaded him not only to abandon the Apostles project but, for a while, choral music generally.

With the country at war, many of the festivals had been suspended. He wrote his last choral work – *The Spirit of England* – again to a secular text, in memory of the fallen from his former county regiment, ('The Worcesters'). With this work, and *The Music Makers,* he was again back in the more familiar realms of setting complete texts taken from those whose whole life revolved around words and not music. It was also much less demanding for an aged composer than to devise his own.

He was, by now, tired and ill. Yet his setting of three diverse war poems had much success following the premiere in 1917, and at Leeds he was urged by the festival authorities to write the third Apostles oratorio for them. Pressure from Henry Embleton, the Festival Chairman, had started some two years before but Elgar had explained at that time that: 'he had . . . intentions about 3rd part of *The Apostles* when the war should be happily over.'[90] He could not contemplate it in 1917 either, and by the time the offer was renewed in 1920, with a £500 'loan' for completing the work, Elgar was in deep mourning for his wife, who had died in April that year. All hope for anything had now gone. The Leeds Festival authorities gently persisted with their request but he had composed nothing since the Cello Concerto, completed in 1919. Working on the project might have been a way of diverting Elgar's attention, for in May 1921 he confided to his friend Troyte Griffith: 'it is possible I may be finishing the III part of *The Apostles* & want to be quiet and uninterrupted generally . . . what I feel now is that I am not young! and want to complete the great work.'[91]

There was a slight revival of his interest in 1922, when Elgar conducted a, by now, rare performance of *The Apostles* and *The Kingdom* side by side at the Three Choirs Festival. But without the support of his wife it was a prospect he could not face alone. The failure was with him still and he wrote movingly to Ivor Atkins: 'I should have destroyed it all.'[92]

Performances of his music, for some reason, declined. By 1922 *The Apostles,* particularly, seemed to be very much out of favour. A performance by the Leeds Choral Union on 8 June was played to a half-empty Queen's Hall. Springing to the attack about public apathy, Bernard Shaw wrote to *The Musical Times* complaining of 'living in a country where the capacity and tastes of schoolboys and sporting costermongers are the measure of a metropolitan culture'.[93] The editor added a note in the published version pointing out that Thursday afternoons in June traditionally supported cricket at Lord's or The Oval and that accordingly it was unfair to expect a 'disengaged body of oratorio lovers to attend the Queen's Hall.'[94] By the following year the position had become even worse. Heated correspondence over several weeks, in October 1923, both in the *Daily Telegraph* and the *Musical Times*, told its own story. The symphonies were being deleted from the orchestral repertoire, to the alarm of Elgar's friends and supporters but to the seeming indifference of the musical public. In these years he composed almost nothing, yet still could not let the idea of completing the trilogy go. Friends tried to persuade him, most notably W. H. ('Billy') Reed, who recalled from 1925:

W.H. ('Billy') Reed with Elgar

'I tried very hard in these days to induce him to work on Part III of the Trilogy; but he did not show any enthusiasm, and always said, "Oh, no one wants any more of that nowadays"; but he would nevertheless sit down at the piano and play portions of it; and the old light would come into his eyes as he worked himself up and began grunting away to himself, with his hands meanwhile flying about the piano. He never could sustain the mood, however, and could not face the drudgery of putting it on paper. The mainspring was broken somehow. I say somehow, because even now it is not certain whether he was disabled by the beginnings of his physical breakdown or by a loss of faith in any real necessity for any more oratorios. He never talked about his religion.'[95]

An approach was made by the Gramophone Company to the Dean and Chapter of Worcester Cathedral – where Elgar was to conduct both *The Apostles* and *The Kingdom* during the 1926 Three Choirs Festival – for the oratorios to be recorded by the new 'electrical process'. Permission was denied and the only recording of Elgar conducting any of the Apostles trilogy music is that of the Prelude to *The Kingdom* recorded in EMI's No.1 Studio at Abbey Road, London, with the BBC Symphony Orchestra on 11 April 1933. A previous recording of the Prologue to *The Apostles* from the Opening Service of the 1927 Three Choirs Festival in Hereford Cathedral with the Festival Chorus and the London Symphony Orchestra, again conducted by Elgar, was subsequently destroyed by EMI because of 'unacceptable recording quality'.[96]

The Leeds Festival authorities tried again to persuade him into writing the third oratorio in 1928. Elgar had been successfully associated with the festival for many years and they wanted a work to mark the retirement of Henry Coward, the Leeds Choral Union's conductor. Elgar declined the invitation. In 1929, after hearing a performance of Vaughan Williams's *Sancta Civitas* ('The Holy City'), he told the composer that: 'I had once thought of setting the words myself, but I shall never do so now.'[97] Others had also tried to persuade him over the years but his heart was never in it. Although he had told August Jaeger in the summer of 1908 that his sketches for Part Three – 'the biggest [part] of all'[98] – were well advanced, no one ever saw them.

There was a final approach from Leeds at the end of 1929 that predictably produced nothing. In the end Elgar had to repay the £500 'loan' of 1921 to the executors of the Leeds Festival Chairman. Henry Embleton had championed Elgar's music but almost bankrupted himself in the process. Elgar, whose friend he was, could not, it seems, persuade anyone that the 'loan' had later been made a gift.

In his final years, and with his health failing, Elgar composed very little which was eventually published. Although he conducted performances of *The Apostles* and *The Kingdom,* this became increasingly difficult for him. Sir Keith Falkner recalled a rehearsal for *The Apostles,* which was to open the 1930 Three Choirs Festival at Hereford:

> 'Elgar took the piano rehearsal in the Close. All went normally until the Judas solo of his betrayal. Judas begins his marvellous song of anguish in which, to quote Elgar, "a proud sinner is swayed by all sorts of feelings" while he sings to music that ranks among the most movingly intense that Elgar ever wrote. Norman [Allin] was halfway through, singing magnificently. Elgar burst into tears. Leaning on the piano he said, "I can't go on". The rehearsal stopped. I have never seen him in such an emotional state. Whenever I hear this great aria now I'm reminded of that occasion.'[99]

Although Elgar never made any real attempt to complete the trilogy many of the sketches for the work – which may have been called *The Last Judgement* – found their way into the music he was working on during his later years, particularly an unfinished opera, *The Spanish Lady,* and the projected Third Symphony. But the Apocalypse, with its Dante-type terrors, never was Elgar's subject. It represented the ending of time and to Elgar music always remained an 'art in time'.

If anything, Elgar appears, in the two completed oratorios of the trilogy, to be a most civilised, reflective, gentle spirit pondering deeply and trying to make sense of an enormous subject. His original vision encompassed a much longer sequence than he was able to accomplish. Had he been 'successful' in his ambition the result might well have been somewhat 'flabby'.

On his deathbed Elgar once again copied out a theme which he had often referred to as 'The Judgement'. This would have started the Prologue to the final oratorio. He gave the scrap of paper to his friend Billy Reed with the words "This is the end, Billy".[100] It was only later that Reed realised Elgar meant the end of his creative life not, as had been supposed, the end of the Third Symphony on which he was still working.

There may, of course, be a more mundane explanation. Elgar was always concerned about his financial situation, which seemed to get ever more precarious as the years progressed. In December 1907 he wrote to Novello: 'I am sadly disappointed with the commercial results of the last oratorios, and for the sake of my people must not waste more time in attempting to write high "felt" music.'[101] The tone was similar when he wrote to August Jaeger in June 1908: 'I am not allowed to beg a dispensation of benevolent providence who objects to the world being saved or purified or improved by a mere musician . . . I cannot afford, for the sake of others, to waste any more time on it. Alas!'[102]

The artistic reasons are more difficult to identify, although it is possible to conclude that Elgar had actually exhausted all his inspiration for the project. The very many less than acceptable performances, including several conducted by Elgar himself, may well have been a disincentive to writing more.

In 1957, the year of Elgar's centenary, Alan Kirby, a choral conductor familiar with *The Apostles* and *The Kingdom,* recounted an incident from early in 1933 when Elgar conducted *The Apostles* for the last time:

> 'Elgar became more and more lost in the music. A slow smile came over his face, and he almost stopped conducting: his spirit seemed to have taken wings. Had it not been for the usual alertness of [his friend] Billy Reed, who was leading the orchestra, and who literally kept the performance together until Elgar came out of his dream, there might have been a complete breakdown. When Elgar left the rostrum it was obvious that he was greatly moved.'[103]

Did his mind momentarily go back to the completion of the full score, in 1903, and to Longdon Marsh, where much of the work was conceived? Or was it the strange inscription on the score from William Morris's *The Earthly Paradise:*

> To what a Heaven and Earth might grow
> If fear beneath the Earth were laid
> If hope failed not, nor love decayed.

Was this still his hope, despite the sense of failure that he experienced over the two completed oratorios of his gigantic projected Apostles trilogy? Was his perception of failure, set against the reality of his shining inspiration and actual achievement, valid? Elgar has left his audiences an infinitely interesting question that cannot be dismissed easily.

PART TWO

All earthly pomp or beauty to express
Is but to carve in snow, on waves to write.
Celestial things, though men conceive them less,
Yet fullest are they in themselves of light.

To Music Bent is my Retired Mind – Thomas Campion

A DETAILED LOOK AT THE APOSTLES TRILOGY

CHAPTER EIGHT

ELGAR'S TEXT FOR
THE APOSTLES TRILOGY

The difficulty of producing his own adequate libretto had prevented Elgar from seriously considering an oratorio on the Apostles theme in response to the Birmingham Festival commission for 1900. This problem had not been resolved when he accepted the commission for the 1903 Festival, and initially lay at the heart of the difficulties Elgar experienced in completing *The Apostles,* and later *The Kingdom* for the 1906 Festival.

It is clear that Elgar had a beginning and an ending in mind for the whole project. What he did not have, before starting work, was any complete idea about what should be included and, perhaps more importantly, excluded from such a vast concept, which was almost an attempt to set the whole New Testament to music. By the time he completed the second work of the projected trilogy Elgar knew he had failed. The two oratorios together did not even cover the ground originally proposed for the first of them.

When Elgar began the trilogy he seemed convinced that the libretto should be largely based on the Authorized version of the Bible. Some text could also be taken from the Revised Standard Version with recourse to the Apocrypha. He was concerned that the text should be perceived from the Anglican viewpoint because of problems that had ensued with the overtly Catholic sentiments in Cardinal Newman's poem that he abridged for *The Dream of Gerontius.* These included the prayers addressed to Mary and the Saints that are actual references based upon the traditions of the Church but denied by Anglicans.

Canon Gorton offered to write an 'Interpretation' of *The Apostles* specifically concentrating on the Anglican aspects. Elgar readily agreed and eventually persuaded Novello to publish it. His initial letter to them, in July 1903, concerning Canon Gorton's offer, made his own anxieties about the acceptance of *The Apostles* as universal quite clear: 'I really think a sort of article wd. do good for many reasons: I have "made" the libretto myself & there are some people (Inter alia the gentlemen who made mischief over *The Light of Life* &, later, over *Gerontius* at Worcester) who are only too anxious to pull it to pieces and say I have treated it solely from the R. Catholic point of view ... Canon Gorton writes so clearly and beautifully.'[104] Elgar's reference to problems with *The Dream of Gerontius* at Worcester is based on the insistence by the Cathedral clergy that all Roman Catholic references had to be deleted from the first Three Choirs Festival performance in 1902. It was to be many years before the work was given either complete or unaltered in an Anglican cathedral.

Surrounding himself with a vast number of theological books and Bible commentaries, he laboriously assembled the text; sometimes whole verses, sometimes a line or even a single phrase to give exactly the emphasis he wanted at each point. But this was improvisation on a grand scale and, given the time constraints, perhaps not the best way of working. Other texts helped Elgar to shape the story, and among the most important of these were Edward Robinson's *Harmony of the Four Gospels*

THE KINGDOM   PART I.

I N T R O D U C T I O N

(Orchestra)

----oOo----

I. JERUSALEM.--- In the Upper Room.

                    The DISCIPLES & the HOLY WOMEN.
Matt.6,33.   Seek first the Kingdom of God,
                    and His righteousness.

                            PETER
Dan.4,1.   Peace be multiplied unto you.

                    The DISCIPLES & the HOLY WOMEN.
I Chron.12,18.   Peace;
                    peace be unto thee,
                            and peace be to thine helpers.

--------oOo---------

Matt.18,20.   "Where two or three are gathered together
                    in My Name,
                    there am I in the midst of them.

                    MARY, M. MAGDALEN, JOHN & PETER.
Acts 20,35.   Remember the words of the Lord Jesus,---

                    The DISCIPLES & the HOLY WOMEN.
Acts 3,14.   Jesus,the Holy One.

"THE RIGHT WRITER IS THE WILLIAMS TYPEWRITER." 57 HOLBORN VIADUCT, LONDON.

Libretto notes for the opening of 'The Kingdom'.

43

(for the narrative aspects of the text); William Henry Pinnock's *An Analysis of New Testament History* and A. E. Hillard's *A Continuous Narrative of Life of Christ in the Words of the Four Gospels* (for the overall scheme); Archbishop Whately's *Lectures on the Characters of Our Lord's Apostles*; Ernest Renan's *The Apostles* (to help with portraying the characters Elgar selected) and Henry Latham's *Pastor pastorum* (for the definitive Acts of the Apostles). The other major reference point was Henry W. Longfellow's narrative poem 'The Divine Tragedy', which Elgar used as a guide through the vast amount of other material he had amassed. He continually clarified his thinking by using Alexander Cruden's *A Complete Concordance to the Old and New Testament* and involved his wife, Alice, in detailed research. Eventually Elgar also decided to use extracts from the Talmud. Alfred Kalisch, the critic, put him in touch with Rabbi F. L. Cohen, who was regarded as perhaps the greatest authority on Jewish ritual and music in England. From Cohen, Elgar obtained not only text but also significant musical sources. Finally he continually used the 35 volumes of the *Encyclopaedia Britannica,* given to him as a present in a special revolving case at Christmas 1902.

An interesting example of this text improvisation was provided by Dora Penny (Dorabella of the 'Enigma Variations') in her book *Edward Elgar: Memories of a Variation,* when she recalled a visit to the Elgars in the middle of February 1903:

> '. . . the study seemed to be full of Bibles. He [Elgar] had a Bible open on the table in front of him and there seemed to be a Bible on every chair and even one on the floor. "Goodness!" I said. "What a collection of Bibles! What have you got there besides the Authorized and Revised Versions?" "I don't know; they've been lent to me. I say, d'you know that the Bible is a most wonderfully interesting book?" "Yes," I said, "I know it is." "What do you know about it? Oh, I forgot, perhaps you do know something about it. [She was, in fact, a clergyman's daughter.] Anyway, I've been reading a lot of it lately and have been quite absorbed." He appeared to be looking out texts and I offered to help. "I want something to fit in here" – pointing to a line [where Christ sang "Blessed are they which do hunger and thirst after righteousness; for they shall be filled."] I thought for a moment and fortunately something suitable occurred to me and I quoted it. ["Mercy and truth are met together: righteousness and peace have kissed each other."] "You don't mean to tell me that comes in the Bible? Show it to me?" I found the eighty-fifth Psalm in one of the Bibles and laid it before him. "Well! That's extraordinary! It's just what I want here".'[105]

This was, of course, less than seven months before the first performance of *The Apostles* when all the text should have been chosen, the music almost composed and at least partly orchestrated. But he was still gathering material at that point, even, as can be seen, from his friends and trying to shape the libretto exactly as he wanted. Working in this way and against time left no space to rethink or replan. There was no sense of an overview. He later tried to explain this method as follows:

'When I propose such a work as this I first of all read everything I can lay my hands on which bears on the subject directly or indirectly, meditating on all that I have sifted out as likely to serve my purpose, and blending it with my musical conceptions. Every personality appears to me in musical dress. I suppose that all who read novels form mental pictures of the characters. So with me: I involuntarily give to each a musical character, clothe each with a musical expression, in the case of Judas, Peter and the rest. I do not seek for character motives; they come, in all places, at all seasons. I never sit down and say; "Now I will compose". The thing is inconceivable to me. What comes, comes of itself.'[106]

But Elgar's only experience with librettos up to that point had been by skilfully adapting existing material. Writing his own, against a tight deadline, was quite another matter.

The original scheme approved by the Birmingham Festival authorities opened with Christ reading a prophesy from Isaiah in the Synagogue and finished with the establishment of the Church at Antioch. Elgar noted many references from his sources: 'the Apostles of the Gospels — striving amongst themselves who should be greatest, looking for the restoration of the Kingdom of Israel, and dismayed at the apprehension of their Master — were trained to become the Apostles of the Acts'; 'in a thousand little occurrences of their wayfaring daily life' (underlined by Elgar).[107] His first indication about the beginning of the oratorio is to be found in a pencilled note in the margin of Pinnock's section 321, 'Christ at Nazareth', where the word 'Begin' is written.[108]

Titles for other sections came from the same source. 'Christ discourses by the way' is an example of where the composer has underlined the last three words and added '-side'[109] which creates Scene Two of *The Apostles*. The book is annotated throughout but the ending of the original *Apostles* scheme,

---

Luke iv. 15—30.

321. Christ at Nazareth.—Jesus then proceeded to Nazareth, where He had been brought up, and as His custom was, entered into the synagogue on the Sabbath-day, and stood up to read; the book of the prophet Esaias, was delivered unto Him, and He read

319. Who were the first disciples called? Where did our Lord begin His preaching? 320. *What was the Second Miracle of our Lord?* 321. What occurred to our Lord when He preached at Nazareth?

Begin.

Elgar's original starting point
(Pinnock's section 321)

as submitted to the Birmingham authorities, is to be found at Pinnock's section 464, 'Success of the Church', where 'the disciples of our <u>Lord were called Christians</u>'.[110] The margin note here simply reads 'end'[111] but as work progressed it became clear that it could not be completed in time. The forced revisions would eventually take two completed oratorios almost less than half this distance.

Elgar originally chose to portray three apostles – Peter, John and Judas – by comparing and contrasting their highly individual characters. This was to be done mainly by reporting their actions rather than by dialogue. But his problem really lay in the portrayal of Christ, who could be seen, in some ways, as central at least to the earlier parts of the story. As the trilogy was a story predominantly about the followers of Christ, however, He could not be allowed to dominate. In the end His character is kept well away from the action – even a prayer sketched out for Christ in the oratorio's earliest scene ('In the mountain, night') was abandoned in favour of an orchestral tone picture. The momentous Christ-centred events which *The Apostles* sets out to portray – the Betrayal, Peter's denial, the Crucifixion and the Resurrection – are passed over with little comment from any of the characters. This is a distancing which can actually get in the way for audiences trying to really believe in the characters as people, either human or divine.

By compiling his libretto in this highly individualistic way, Elgar became much too involved in it and appears to have moved very little further than his nineteenth-century predecessors in creating oratorio texts. He had often held up Handel's *Messiah* as a powerful influence on his religious

Elgar's original ending point
(Pinnock's section 464)

46

choral-music writing. A comparison of this single work with Elgar's projected Apostles trilogy shows that Handel's oratorio was also a study of the early days of the Christian faith, finishing with Revelation. Jennens's libretto for Handel may well succeed because it lacks intricate detail, leaving space for real musical development. Elgar's misjudgement with the texts for *The Apostles* and *The Kingdom* is that they are, perhaps, too detailed, leading to congestion, stifling the music's natural development. August Jaeger, in his published analysis of both oratorios, seeks to make a virtue out of the detail Elgar used. This served only to further confuse matters in the public's mind and cause Elgar a great deal of consternation.

In an introduction for a projected, but eventually unpublished, edition of *The Apostles* libretto, Elgar wrote:

'The Prologue & division I (The Calling) & II (By the Wayside) explain themselves: in the remainder of the work the following sequence of ideas was present in my mind when compiling the text.

I   That forgiveness of sins must be shown to the prospective teachers: Mary Magdalene is the most important type: a sinner who truly repents, not in old age, but in the flower of life, the sinner who in the deepest distress pleads for mercy & does not "fall from her hope in the Lord".

II   A manifestation of Christ's supernatural powers was necessary to my plan. I chose the miracle of Walking on the waters in preference to the Transfiguration because all the Apostles were present at the former.

III   No attempt to depict the foundation of the Church could be considered in any sense adequate which did not deal largely with the traitor: Judas, the type of sinner who despairs, is given prominence not from any melodramatic reason but because the lesson to be learnt from him is needed more at the present day than at any other time. Avarice & unbridled ambition leading to atheism and despair, sometimes ending in self-destruction may be found too often in this meeting time of centuries.'[112]

CHAPTER NINE

ELGAR'S MUSICAL IDEAS
FOR THE APOSTLES TRILOGY

The musical construction of the two oratorios is largely based on *leitmotif* or representative themes – a system which Wagner had used to telling effect in the operas of *Der Ring des Nibelungen*. Composers before Wagner had employed this very obvious device where themes represent a person, natural element or abstract idea and are used whenever these persons, elements or ideas recur throughout a work. Their importance in the Apostles trilogy lies in their emotional significance. Elgar himself indicated that 'the music, by use of *leitmotifs,* makes much allusion clear which must escape when the words are read only.'[113] He explained this method in a letter to Canon Gorton: 'as I said before, the music explains – by means of *leitmotifs* & general treatment – much of the interdependence of the words.'[114] Great composers are able to use *leitmotif* with considerable flexibility and subtlety, Elgar amongst them: 'I really do it without thought, intuitively I mean'[115] he said on one occasion. His use of *leitmotif*, especially in the orchestral accompaniment, often tells the listener what a character is really thinking in spite of what they may actually be singing.

August Jaeger wrote analytical and descriptive notes for both oratorios. For *The Apostles* he identified more than 60 themes and for *The Kingdom* almost 30, to which he applied titles. He also identified more than 70 other themes from both works but was unable to give them descriptive titles. His preoccupation with identifying the thematic material became a real obsession which caused Elgar some concern because the composer wanted audiences to listen to the music as music without being distracted trying to identify themes by name. Some are not themes in the true sense of the word, even though they are repeated on more than one occasion throughout the works. Elgar was, of course, right to be concerned, as Jaeger had unwittingly given commentators and critics alike an impression that the works were made up of a jigsaw of fragments rather than looking at the relationship of those fragments. Ernest Newman, especially, pointed as an example, and with undisguised glee, to Jaeger's description of a little figure of three notes that occurs many times in Scene III of *The Apostles* (subtitled – 'There arose a great tempest in the sea') as 'the ship'. He wrote: "the Ship" motive is no more suggestive of a ship than it is of a banana or a motor-car!'[116]

Elgar appears not to have been as successful in the use of *leitmotif* in *The Apostles* and *The Kingdom* as he was in *The Dream of Gerontius*. There, a smaller number of themes, appearing mainly in the Prelude, are fully developed orchestrally in a context which, when they are eventually given words, assume a natural and understandable significance for the listener. In the two completed works of the trilogy, themes are representative at their point of first entry but can become stale with so much repetition. By using Jaeger's analysis the following becomes clear:

Untitled thematic material *The Apostles* 27 themes
The Kingdom 47 themes

Titled thematic material	*The Apostles* 66 themes
	The Kingdom 29 themes
Bars in completed works	*The Apostles* 1939
	The Kingdom 1399
Untitled examples used	*The Apostles* 56 times = once every 35 bars average
	The Kingdom 87 times = once every 16 bars average
Titled examples used	*The Apostles* 338 times = once every 6 bars average
	The Kingdom 185 times = once every 8 bars average
Overall use of themes	*The Apostles* 394 times = once every 5 bars average
	The Kingdom 272 times = once every 5 bars average

Throughout the two oratorios the orchestral scoring is, for the most part, innovative and of great beauty but it is quite clear from a study of the sketches that the prominence of the orchestra is at the expense of the vocal line. Often the orchestral part (representing a *leitmotif*) is written in ink, whereas the voice part is in pencil. Perhaps the most striking example of this is in the Virgin Mary's soliloquy, 'The Sun Goeth Down', where the word 'patience' is used twice and written – in pencil – an octave lower. The orchestra – written in ink – is occupied with the major theme for 'Christ's loneliness'. The final version of the solo has the voice soaring by a seventh at this point but this may well have been an afterthought prompted by August Jaeger and not originally intended.

Elgar had discovered two Gregorian chants at the home of his friend Adrian Mignot in Liverpool in November 1902 when he was, belatedly, beginning to give real consideration to the first oratorio due for the Birmingham Festival, then less than twelve months away. Searching for a definitive theme, hopefully based on a Gregorian chant, to represent all the Apostles collectively, had produced nothing. Then, following a normal Sunday morning church service, his friend Alfred Rodewald recalled: he [Elgar] was sitting at a writing table and aimlessly put his hand upon the page of a book lying there. He looked and saw that his hand was resting upon a Gregorian chant. This, he saw immediately, was the theme that had been eluding him.'[117] What he had discovered was part of the

The Gradual 'Constitues eos'

Gradual *Constitues eos* and much of the named thematic material in *The Apostles* can be clearly traced to this. The second discovery was the Antiphon *O sacrum convivium* from the Second Vespers of the Feast of Corpus Christi.

O . sa - crum Con - vi - vi - um, in quo . . Chri-stus . . su mi - tur ;

The Antiphon 'O Sacrum Convivium'

While both of these chants were originally to be used in *The Apostles,* because of the drastic revisions to this work, the Antiphon is only associated with the music for Peter in *The Kingdom,* although much of this was written during the early part of his work on what later became *The Apostles.* The first harmonisation of the Antiphon appears in Elgar's sketchbook eleven with a very self-critical comment appended. He simply wrote 'too sentimental'.[118]

CHAPTER TEN

COMPARISONS WITH
'THE DREAM OF GERONTIUS'

The two completed oratorios of the Apostles trilogy have inevitably suffered over the years by being compared with *The Dream of Gerontius*. However unfair this may be, it is as well to consider the reasons. *The Apostles* and *The Kingdom* were acknowledged, from the start, by Elgar as oratorios. *Gerontius* never was an oratorio, a point which Elgar made to August Jaeger on more than one occasion: 'there is no word invented yet to describe it.'[119] He had a particular horror of 'that dreadful term — a sacred cantata'[120] and felt that the work could not really be classified as anything conventional in musical terms. What *The Dream of Gerontius* represents is the highest development of Elgar's choral works based on sagas — *The Black Knight*, *King Olaf* and *Caractacus* — on which he had worked between 1892 and 1898. Thus it could be seen as the end of a phase in the composer's development, whereas *The Apostles* and *The Kingdom* are part of another development that culminated in the First Symphony. When Sir Adrian Boult originally recorded *The Kingdom* he wrote the following note by way of an introduction:

> 'I know that critics differ considerably in comparing the three great oratorios which Elgar has left us. The majority back *Gerontius* and would say it is a pity that he never reached those heights again. I am afraid I disagree. I think there is a great deal in *The Kingdom* that is more than a match for *Gerontius*, and I feel that it is a much more balanced work and throughout maintains a stream of glorious music, whereas *Gerontius* has its ups and downs. Perhaps I was prejudiced by hearing a great friend of Elgar's (who was very kind to me in my young days) [Frank Schuster] jump down the throat of a young man who made this criticism: "My dear boy, beside *The Kingdom*, *Gerontius* is the work of a raw amateur." '[121]

While this may be unfair, it illustrates the point about Elgar's development as a composer.

There are weaknesses in all three works, but *Gerontius* has a more immediate impact because of the single idea on which Cardinal Newman's text is founded — the journey of a man's soul from death to judgement and beyond. This provides a unity of emotion to which Elgar responded in a way he found himself incapable of doing in either *The Apostles* or *The Kingdom*. They are, almost consciously, words set to music in a way that *The Dream of Gerontius* does not appear to be. But, again this is perhaps unfair. The subjects of these works are very different, for the power that drives *The Dream of Gerontius* would have been entirely misplaced in less personal works about the founding of the early Church. Yet here the sheer scope of the story demanded music approached in a different way. If some critics, after the first performance of *The Apostles*, were of the opinion that it was something of an advance from *The Dream of Gerontius,* they were on the right lines. Elgar's harmonic language and his style in constructing this vast work had dramatically changed to a twentieth-century approach.

The critic Ernest Newman was perhaps more perceptive and far-sighted, given the difficulties Elgar experienced with the librettos for *The Apostles* and *The Kingdom* when he wrote, in December 1901:

> 'He [Elgar] has been held back by the ideals of the musical generation now on the verge of extinction . . . I say nothing of the reasons, other than artistic, for Dr Elgar writing so many cantatas and oratorios. If the road to success lies through the bog of the Festivals [the 'bog' referred to here was an Anglican one], a composer must needs take that path; but he cannot do so without wasting a good deal of his time and strength as an artist, and without a quantity of undesirable substance clinging to him for some time after . . . There can, of course, be no question that Gerontius is not only the finest work ever produced at an English Festival, but the finest work Dr Elgar has written. It is, indeed, the real Elgar, the Elgar that has been made by his heredity, his reading, his reflection upon life, the Elgar one knows in the flesh and the spirit. But Gerontius is so great because Dr Elgar has had the rare good fortune to come into contact, at the very height of his powers as a musician and as a thinker, with a poem particularly fitted to stimulate and become part of him. <u>I very much doubt whether he will be so fortunate again.</u>'[122]

Of the two works, *The Apostles* outshines *The Kingdom* for dramatic scenes – but the second work is more unified and less fragmentary. It is performed more often perhaps for this reason. The basic problem in both oratorios is their reliance on a *leitmotif* structure. Often these are used with sensitivity, but on many occasions their use to underline the text seriously interrupts the flow of the music. Elgar once made a remark to August Jaeger about *Gerontius* where he maintained that: 'if the words are sufficiently interesting, the music will do.'[123] This is oddly at variance with his pre-occupation in the completed oratorios of the Apostles trilogy where the text was always expected to grow out of the musical ideas. Sometimes, however, these works produce words set to music in a somewhat mechanistic way. They remain highly original at their best moments and perhaps in none of Elgar's other music are so many of his strengths *and* weaknesses revealed.

CHAPTER ELEVEN

'THE APOSTLES'
op. 49 IN MORE DETAIL

In *The Apostles* Elgar used one of his largest orchestras. There are parts for bass clarinet and double bassoon with the organ, for the first time in a major Elgar work, assuming an important part independent of doubling the chorus. The shofar, a Jewish liturgical instrument made of ram's horn, is represented by an additional trumpet (straight [without valves] if possible) and the percussion section is augmented with gongs (small and large), antique cymbals, glockenspiel, tambourine and triangle. Although two harps are specified, the second is optional.

Elgar's use of the orchestra is arguably more important than in *The Dream of Gerontius* and contributes greatly to the overall effect, often setting the scene, against which the characters stand out in sharp relief.

There are parts for seven soloists:

The Blessed Virgin - Soprano	The Angel - Soprano	Mary Magdalene - Contralto
St John - Tenor	St Peter - Bass	Judas - Bass
Jesus - Bass		

Elgar's original intention for an eighth soloist (Thomas) was abandoned as impractical when the scope of the oratorio had to be drastically reduced. Some sketches exist for the 'Thomas incident' (his doubts about the truth of the Resurrection), although not worked out in any detail.

A large, mixed chorus is required and sometimes split into a chorus and semi-chorus. Elgar's later experiences in conducting performances of *The Apostles* led him to suggest that only 'a few voices' from the chorus should sing at various points. At a performance of the oratorio in Hereford during the 1921 Three Choirs Festival he employed a semi-chorus of nine men to make up the twelve Apostles — Peter, John and Judas being soloists.

The libretto contains very little narrative except where necessary to explain the context of a scene and this is sung usually by the tenor soloist, occasionally by the contralto or a unison chorus. Wherever possible the story is continued by the characters themselves. Elgar caused his publishers some consternation by insisting on the exact layout of the solo lines in both the vocal and full scores. Jesus, when he appeared, had to have the top line; the two bass soloists — Peter and Judas — should always have separate staves, even if they were singing together; the prefix 'St.' (Saint) was removed quite late in the already complicated printing schedule and he became very precise about the exact indentations required when the libretto was typeset.

Following major revisions to his original scheme Elgar abandoned further composition of *The Apostles* which left the work with a Prologue and seven scenes.

PROLOGUE

(*Chorus and Orchestra*) The Spirit of the Lord is upon me, because He hath anointed me to preach the Gospel to the poor: He hath sent me to heal the broken-hearted, to preach deliverance to the captives and recovery of sight to the blind – to preach the acceptable year of the Lord; to give unto them that mourn a garland for ashes, the oil of joy for mourning, the garment of praise for the spirit of heaviness; that they might be called the trees of righteousness, the planting of the Lord, that He might be glorified. For as the earth bringeth forth her bud, and as the garden that causeth the things that are sown in it to spring forth; so the Lord God will cause righteousness and praise to spring forth before all the nations. The Spirit of the Lord is upon me, because He hath anointed me to preach the Gospel.

The Prologue contains a number of themes that are important not only in *The Apostles* but also in *The Kingdom*. Elgar also used a semi-autobiographical quotation from his earlier cantata *The Light of Life* – a work that tells, in essence, how sight was restored to a blind man. In the Prologue to *The Apostles* there is a reference, from Isaiah, to the recovery of sight and Elgar immediately takes us back to his earlier work by giving a direct musical quotation. This was a device that he appropriately employed in other works.

Elgar's method of text assembly, at least in the early stages of the oratorio's composition, can be seen from the first draft of the Prologue and Scene I – 'The Calling of the Apostles'. Although he had a usable text (the quotation of the Isaiah prophesy) he fashioned the version for the Prologue from several sources. Luke's translation of Isaiah was more acceptable to Elgar than the original, but he reverted to the Old Testament version when the gospel writer's quotation ran out by adding a single word from the Revised Standard Bible (Isaiah 61:3) substituting the words 'garland for ashes' in place of 'beauty for ashes'. He edited out Isaiah 61:6, 'Ye shall be named the priests of the Lord; men shall call you the Ministers of our God', but used this later in a chorus from Scene I of the oratorio. This careful use of material from texts already considered was, at that stage, typical of his approach to forming the libretto. Time constraints meant, however, that overall such a complicated method of working had eventually to be abandoned.

It is in the Prologue that the first multiple repetition of themes becomes evident. This was to be the very characteristic that put at risk, and may have partially devalued, both *The Apostles* and *The Kingdom* with its listeners. The choral writing, though, is assured and supported by some innovative orchestration.

The 1903 Birmingham Triennial Festival Programme Book

Programme.

WEDNESDAY MORNING, OCTOBER 14TH, 1903.

ORATORIO .... "THE APOSTLES" .... *Edward Elgar.*

(PARTS I. & II.) **Op. 49.**

First time of Performance. (Conducted by the Composer.)

THE BLESSED VIRGIN AND THE ANGEL (Soprano)	MADAME ALBANI.
MARY MAGDALENE (Contralto)	MISS MURIEL FOSTER.
ST. JOHN (Tenor)	MR JOHN COATES.
ST. PETER (Bass)	MR. KENNERLEY RUMFORD.
JUDAS (Bass)	MR. ANDREW BLACK.
JESUS (Bass)	MR. FFRANGCON-DAVIES.

PART I.

PROLOGUE.

CHORUS .. .. .. The Spirit of the Lord is upon me.

I.—THE CALLING OF THE APOSTLES.

RECIT. TENOR .. .. And it came to pass.

IN THE MOUNTAIN—NIGHT.

Orchestra.
SOPRANO SOLO (*The Angel Gabriel*) The voice of Thy watchman.

THE DAWN.

CHORUS, ALTO & TENOR (*The Watchers on the Temple roof*). It shines!

MORNING PSALM.

CHORUS .. .. .. It is a good thing to give thanks unto the Lord.
RECIT. TENOR .. .. And when it was day.
CHORUS .. .. .. The Lord hath chosen them.
SOLI (*John, Peter, and Judas*) We are the servants of the Lord.
SOLO (*The Angel*) .. Thy watchmen shall lift up the voice.

II.—BY THE WAYSIDE.

SOLO, QUASI RECIT. (*Jesus*) Blessed are the poor in spirit.
SOLI (*The Blessed Virgin, John, Peter, and Judas*) He setteth the poor on high from affliction.
CHORUS .. .. .. Weeping may endure for a night.

III.—BY THE SEA OF GALILEE.

RECIT. TENOR .. .. And straightway Jesus constrained His disciples.

IN MAGDALA.

SOLO (*Mary Magdalene*) O Lord Almighty, God of Israel.
CHORUS (FANTASY) .. Let us fill ourselves with costly wine.
SOLO (*Mary Magdalene*) Is Thy wrath against the sea?
SEMI-CHORUS (*The Apostles*) It is a Spirit.
SOLO (*Jesus*) .. .. Be of good cheer.
SOLO (*Peter*) .. .. Lord, if it be Thou, bid me come unto Thee.

IN CÆSAREA PHILIPPI.

RECIT. TENOR .. .. When Jesus came into the parts of Cæsarea Philippi.
RECIT. (*Jesus*) .. .. Whom do men say that I, the Son of man, am?
CHORUS .. .. .. Some say, John the Baptist.
SOLO (*Peter*) .. .. Thou art the Christ.
SOLO (*Jesus*) .. .. Blessed art thou, Simon Bar-Jona.
SOLI AND CHORUS .. Proclaim unto them that dwell on the earth.
SOLO (*Jesus*) .. .. And I will give unto thee the keys of the Kingdom of Heaven.
SOLO (*Mary*) .. .. Hearken, O daughter.
RECIT. TENOR .. .. She stood at His feet weeping.
CHORUS OF WOMEN .. This man, if He were a prophet.
SOLO (*Mary Magdalene*) Hide not Thy face far from me.
SOLO (*Jesus*) .. .. Thy sins are forgiven.
SOLI AND CHORUS .. Turn you to the stronghold, ye prisoners of hope.

PART II.

INTRODUCTION (*Orchestra*).

IV.—THE BETRAYAL.

RECIT. TENOR .. .. And it came to pass.
CHORUS .. .. .. I will smite the Shepherd.
SOLO (*Peter*) .. .. Be it far from Thee, Lord.
CHORUS (*the Apostles*) .. Though we should die with Thee.
CHORUS, TENOR & BASS Then gathered the chief Priests and Pharisees.
SOLO (*Judas*) .. .. What are ye willing to give me?
CHORUS, TENOR & BASS And they weighed unto him thirty pieces of silver.
SOLO (*Judas*) .. .. Let Him make speed, and hasten His work.

IN GETHSEMANE.

SOLO (*Judas*) .. .. Hail, Master.
SOLO (*Jesus*) .. .. Whom seek ye?
CHORUS .. .. .. Jesus of Nazareth.
SOLO (*Jesus*) .. .. I am He.
RECIT. CONTRALTO .. And they all forsook Him.
CHORUS .. .. .. And the Lord turned and looked upon Peter.

THE TEMPLE.

RECIT. CONTRALTO .. And Judas, which had betrayed Him.
CHORUS .. .. .. O Lord God, to whom vengeance belongeth.
SOLO (*Judas*) .. .. My punishment is greater than I can bear.

WITHOUT THE TEMPLE.

SOLO (*Judas*) .. .. Whither shall I go from Thy Spirit?
CHORUS .. .. .. Blessed is the man whom Thou chastenest.

V.—GOLGOTHA.

ORCHESTRA .. .. "Eli, Eli, lama sabachthani?"
CHORUS .. .. .. Truly, this was the Son of God.
SOLO (*Mary*) .. .. The sword hath pierced through mine own soul.
SOLO (*John*) .. .. Thou hast trodden the wine press alone.

VI.—AT THE SEPULCHRE.

RECIT. CONTRALTO .. And very early in the morning.
CHORUS, TENOR & BASS The face of all the East.
SEMI-CHORUS, SOPRANO AND CONTRALTO Why seek ye the living?

VII.—THE ASCENSION.

CHORUS (*Apostles*) .. We trusted that it had been He.
SOLO (*Jesus*) .. .. Peace be unto you.
CHORUS (*Apostles*) .. Lord, wilt Thou at this time restore.
SOLO (*Jesus*) .. .. It is not for you to know the time or the seasons.
RECIT. CONTRALTO .. And when He had spoken these things.

IN HEAVEN.

SEMI-CHORUS & CHORUS Alleluia!

ON EARTH.

SOLI & CHORUS .. .. Give us one heart and one way.

Interval of Three Quarters of an Hour between Parts I. and II.

SYMPHONY IN E MINOR (No. 4) .... *Johannes Brahms.*

Op. 98.

Morning Programme, 14 October 1903

PART I

I   THE CALLING OF THE APOSTLES

Recit. (Tenor) And it came to pass in those days that Jesus went out into a mountain to pray, and continued all night in prayer to God.

Elgar's use of the title 'The Calling of the Apostles' is a direct quotation from the heading to Chapter 8 in Latham's book about Christ's education of the Apostles, *Pastor pastorum*. This book had a major influence on the way that the early part of the oratorio was put together. The subtitle of Latham's study – 'The Schooling of the Apostles' – eventually persuaded Elgar away from dealing with this aspect in Scene I and confine the teaching to Scene II, which included the Beatitudes. It was also a way of representing Latham's view about the importance of Christ's somewhat itinerant and wayfaring existence both to the education and development of the Apostles as a group.

A tenor recitative precedes the first of three scenes in this section. Elgar uses no representational themes in this short solo, preferring to start and finish it with a miniature *ritornello*. The recitative is, however, significant simply because of that, and many of the sections in both *The Apostles* and *The Kingdom* are constructed on a similar, but simple, A-B-A scheme. This method becomes immediately apparent in the very next section.

IN THE MOUNTAIN – NIGHT

(ORCHESTRA)

This mysterious and highly effective music, framed by a pastoral melody for cor anglais and two oboes in canon, played *outside* the main orchestra, introduces one of the main *leitmotifs* in *The Apostles*. A four-bar melody (called 'The Prayer of Christ' by August Jaeger in his analysis) derives from the Gregorian Gradual *Constitues eos* and appears at every major climax in the work, being used 13 times but only once in *The Kingdom*.

Although the whole of Scene I is based around Luke 6, Elgar originally inserted other verses, including a prayer for Jesus from John 17: 'I pray for them: I pray not for the world, but for them which Thou hast given me: for they are Thine'. This abandoned sketch has a pencil note 'I am not satisfied with this yet'[124], which may indicate some doubt about proceeding with a different setting of the same text he had used in *The Light of Life* some years before. Too many autobiographical quotes were out of the question as overindulgence on his part. The final version of *The Apostles* has the orchestral prayer substituted.

The Angel Gabriel (Soprano) The voice of Thy watchman! The Lord returneth to Zion – break forth into joy, sing together ye waste places of Jerusalem: for the Lord hath comforted His people.

(ORCHESTRA)

The Angel "Behold My servant, Whom I have chosen; My beloved, in Whom my soul is well pleased: He shall not strive, nor cry aloud: neither shall anyone hear His voice in the streets: a bruised reed shall He not break, the dimly burning wick shall He not quench. and in His name shall the Gentiles hope."

The voice of Thy watchman!

The orchestral accompaniment to the soprano solo of the Angel Gabriel is highly reminiscent of the rising orchestral phrase that introduces the Angel in *The Dream of Gerontius*. Once again Elgar uses a semi-autobiographical approach to his music. The solo itself – which should be sung '<u>distant</u>' – is interrupted by the orchestral development of several motifs already used. At the conclusion of the prophecy the orchestra creates, from the Gregorian Gradual *Constitues eos* and other fragments, the motif that is used most often in the work. This sturdy, diatonic theme, representing *The Apostles* themselves, is used 26 times throughout the work and a further 8 times in *The Kingdom*.

Over a return of the pastoral theme for cor anglais and two oboes the dawn is at last heralded.

THE DAWN

SHOFAR *(distant)*

The Watchers (on the Temple roof) It shines!

(Clang of the Gates – SHOFAR)

The face of all the East is now ablaze with light, the dawn reacheth even unto Hebron!

Elgar's introduction to the first Temple scene by imitating the shofar – a Hebrew trumpet made from ram's horn – is both novel and authentic. Its growing insistence, taken up by the orchestral brass, gradually brightens the music as the Watchers on the Temple roof greet the dawn. The orchestration becomes more excited as the gates of the Temple are opened and the chorus takes up the Morning Psalm (using words from Talmud and Misnah together with Psalm 92). Rabbi Cohen remarked to the composer about the potential use of a real shofar: 'You would startle "The Antagonists" if you introduced one into your orchestra – with a genuine Hebrew to blow it.'[125] But it was Cohen who devised the 'complete flourish' on the instrument imitated in this scene.

Major additions to the section were sketched but later abandoned or used elsewhere. The first was a quotation from Psalm 30: 'Weeping may endure for a night but joy cometh in the morning', which found its way into the Beatitudes section. The others were intended to extend the scene of the Apostles calling and were taken variously from Mark 3:14 plus the long list of all the Apostles by name; a scene of healing which went along with Luke's picture of 'a great multitude of people' hearing Jesus and 'healed of their diseases'. The largest sketch though, is based on II Chronicles 19:11, initially a pencilled afterthought to the actual calling. The chorus 'The Lord hath chosen them' eventually came from this idea, forcing a complete revision of the first libretto draft and moving the Beatitudes into a separate section. This is important, for it illustrates clearly that Elgar's musical creativity quickly exhausted his initial thoughts. The pencilled 'if necy [necessary]'[126] at the head of sketches indicates where he was simply trying to extend scenes already composed. As he began to add more ideas, the sketches took on a larger form and the pencilled note 'omit, if too long, the whole incident on this page'[127], which appears in many places, is telling indeed.

> ### MORNING PSALM
>
> *The Singers (within the Temple)* It is a good thing to give thanks to the Lord, and sing praises unto Thy name, O Most High: to shew forth Thy lovingkindness in the morning, and Thy faithfulness every night, upon the psaltery; upon the harp with a solemn sound. For Thou, Lord, hast made me glad through Thy work: I will triumph in the works of Thy hands. For, lo, Thine enemies, O Lord, shall perish: all the workers of iniquity shall be scattered. The righteous shall flourish like the palm tree: he shall grow like a cedar in Lebanon.

The psalm is set to a traditional Hebrew melody – the second in a set of Hispanic-Mauresque medieval chants, and one of a number edited by Ernest Paur. It appears in an edition of *Traditional Hebrew Melodies* published by Augner. Elgar used traditional material in this Temple scene, in Scene II of *The Kingdom* (where the Holy Women are outside the Beautiful Gate of the Temple) and for the violin solo in Mary's soliloquy ('The Sun Goeth Down') in *The Kingdom*.

(SHOFAR AND ORCHESTRA)

An orchestral depiction of the sunrise, which ends this section, is dazzling in its effect and could be said to more than outshine *The Dream of Gerontius* where the soul goes before God in a similar blaze of light. There are other parallels here with the middle section of the Prelude to *The Dream of Gerontius* and the music follows a similar shape but, once again, in a more dramatic way.

Recit. (Tenor) And when it was day, He called unto Him His disciples: and of them He chose twelve, whom also He named Apostles, that they should be with Him, and that He might send them forth to preach.

Chorus The Lord hath chosen them to stand before Him, to serve Him. He hath chosen the weak to confound the mighty; He will direct their work in truth! Behold! God exalteth by His power, who teacheth like Him? The meek will he guide in judgment, and the meek will He teach His way. He will direct their work in truth, for out of Zion shall go forth the law.

John, Peter and Judas We are the servants of the Lord.

Peter Thou wilt shew us the path of life; in Thy light shall we see light. Let Thy work appear unto Thy servants.

John O blessed are they which love Thee, for they shall rejoice in Thy peace: and shall be filled with the law.

Judas We shall eat of the riches of the Gentiles, and in their glory shall we boast ourselves.

John, Peter and Judas For out of Zion shall go forth the law and the word of the Lord from Jerusalem.

Chorus The Lord hath chosen them, they shall be named the Priests of the Lord, men shall call them the Ministers of our God.

John O blessed are they which love Thee.

Peter In Thy light shall we see light.

Judas God exalteth by His power.

Chorus He will direct their work; they are the servants of the Lord.

The Angel and Chorus Thy watchmen shall lift up the voice; with the voice together shall they sing: for they shall see eye to eye, when the Lord shall bring again Zion.

John, Peter and Judas Come ye, and let us walk in the light of the Lord.

Jesus Behold, I send you forth. He that receiveth you, receiveth Me; and he that receiveth Me, receiveth Him that sent Me.

John, Peter and Judas We are the servants of the Lord.

The Angel Look down from heaven, O God, and behold, and visit this vine.

Chorus Amen.

By careful use of text the individual characters of John, Peter and Judas are introduced in the complex ensemble that follows a brief narration by the tenor soloist about the choosing of the Apostles. It is the first time that we encounter Judas, who plays such an important role in this work and in Elgar's thinking. He is here portrayed as an ambitious man, somewhat dissenting from the tone of the other's utterances, who has not only a true faith in Christ but also a misconception of Christ's power which he perceives can be put to good use on earth. There is more than a hint here of his preoccupation with worldly matters.

II BY THE WAYSIDE

Jesus BLESSED are the poor in spirit: for theirs is the kingdom of heaven

Mary (The Blessed Virgin), John and Peter (He setteth the poor on high from affliction:

Judas He poureth contempt upon princes.)

Jesus BLESSED are they that mourn: for they shall be comforted.

John (The Lord shall give them rest from their sorrow,

Peter and will turn their mourning into joy,

Mary and John and will comfort them: —

Women Weeping may endure for a night

Men but joy cometh in the morning.)

Jesus BLESSED are the meek: for they shall inherit the earth.

The People (The meek shall increase their joy —

Mary, John and Peter in the Lord;

The People and the poor among men shall rejoice —

Mary, John and Peter in the Holy One of Israel.)

Jesus BLESSED are they which do hunger and thirst after righteousness: for they shall be filled.

Mary, John, Peter and Judas (Mercy and truth are met together: righteousness and peace have kissed each other.

The People Sow to yourselves in righteousness, —)

Jesus BLESSED are the merciful: for they shall obtain mercy.

The People (Reap in mercy.

Mary, John and Peter He that hath mercy on the poor, happy is he.

Judas The poor is hated even of his own neighbour: the rich hath many friends.

The People Draw out thy soul to the hungry,

John and satisfy the afflicted soul;

Peter then shall thy light rise in obscurity.)

Jesus BLESSED are the pure in heart: for they shall see God.

Mary (Thou art of purer eyes than to behold evil.

John Blessed are the undefiled.

Peter Who can say, I have made my heart clean?

Judas The stars are not pure in his sight,

The People how much less man.)

Jesus BLESSED are the peacemakers: for they shall be called the children of God.

The People (The work of righteousness shall be peace.)

Jesus BLESSED are they which are persecuted for righteousness sake: for theirs is the kingdom of heaven. Rejoice, and be exceeding glad; for great is your reward in heaven: for so persecuted they the prophets which were before you.

Soli and Chorus Blessed are they which have been sorrowful for all Thy scourges, for they shall rejoice for Thee, when they have seen all Thy glory, and shall be glad for ever.

The short orchestral introduction to the second scene is reminiscent of the Prelude to the second part of *The Dream of Gerontius* in its simple three-part writing. Jesus gives the Beatitudes in a straightforward and unforced way. The comments of the Apostles and Jesus's mother are reflective, the only note of harshness coming, once again, from Judas.

Most of the original libretto for this section was actually planned for the previous scene ('The Calling of the Apostles'). It is based on St. Matthew's Gospel (perhaps in line with Robinson's study *The Harmony of the Four Gospels*) plus the account of Christ reascending the mountain from where he would return to preach the Sermon on the Mount and heal the sick. There appears to have been no idea, in the early stages of composition, to bring out the individual characteristics of the principle Apostles chosen by Elgar. When the separate scene of the Beatitudes was decided upon, the previous section having become overweighted with material, Elgar told Capel-Cure that it was now his intention that the Apostles should 'stand out as living characters'[128] and that the 'character of Christ should remain static. His importance underlined by the simple dignity of his utterances'[129]. This was in sharp contrast to the original idea for Scene I – 'The Calling of the Apostles' – where Christ was the only character, praying to his Father, choosing the Apostles, preaching and healing. Elgar later realised his mistake here and focused his attention more on 'the subjects rather than the King – on the disciples rather than the Master'[130].

Elgar's original plan for a much larger scene had led to him obtaining, from Capel-Cure, a libretto based on the section in Longfellow's poem *The Divine Tragedy* which details Christ moving through villages and fields of corn, blessing children. This text contained the Beatitudes and Elgar, in one of his many forced revisions, condensed the scene again and again because time constraints would not allow its proper development. It was to be the section of the oratorio that attracted much criticism. Elgar's aim was to depict, in a reflective way, Christ giving comfort to people who were poor, ill, weak and starving; their problems weigh on him heavily. Some critics felt however, that this approach lessened the scene's significance because the Beatitudes are universally accepted as of great importance. They also felt that the general impression was a disjointed one, but to the composer this section was of vital importance. In unpublished notes he quoted a sentence from Hillard's *Life of Christ*: 'they [the Beatitudes] sum up the revolution Christ is going to cause in men's ideas of goodness.'[131] As a further commentary he added: 'I have purposely made the listeners interpret the words in many cases too literally, that is, more in accordance with their own feelings at the time than with later enlightenment.'[132] Only eight of the Beatitudes from chapter 5 of St Matthew are set. The ninth, 'Blessed art thou when men shall revile you', was much too close to Elgar's own fears about the survival of his music and later found its way into Mary's soliloquy 'The Sun Goeth Down' in *The Kingdom*.

After his setting of the Beatitudes, Elgar was to have included material from The Sermon on the Mount and sketched this out. It was a sort of jigsaw method of construction that attracted critical comment from those with whom it was discussed. The rejected material allowed a more unified final version to emerge. With so much to do and a shortage of time it might be that Elgar was following the theory that any progress was better than none. When, in a 1905 Birmingham University 'Retrospect' lecture, he was asked to 'illustrate the actual labour of composition' Elgar quoted Tchaikovsky:

'There is no doubt that even the greatest musical geniuses have sometimes worked without inspiration. The guest does not always respond to the first invitation. We must ALWAYS work, and a self-respecting artist must not fold his hands on the pretext that he was not in the mood. If we wait for the mood, without endeavouring to meet it half way, we easily become indolent and apathetic. We must be patient, and believe that inspiration will come to those who can master their disinclination.'[133]

III   BY THE SEA OF GALILEE

Recit. (Tenor) And straightway Jesus constrained His disciples to get into a ship, and go before Him unto the other side: and He went up into a mountain to pray: and when the evening was come, He was there alone. And His disciples went over the sea towards Capernaum.

IN THE TOWER OF MAGDALA

Mary Magdalene O Lord Almighty, God of Israel, the soul in anguish, the troubled spirit, crieth unto Thee. Hear and have mercy; for Thou art merciful: have pity upon me, because I have sinned before Thee. Hear the voice of the forlorn, and deliver me out of my fear. Help me, desolate woman, which have no helper but Thee: Woe is me! for I am as when they have gathered the summer fruits – as the grape-gleanings of the vintage. Have pity upon me, because I have sinned before Thee. My tears run down like a river day and night. Whatsoever mine eyes desired I kept not from them, I withheld not my heart from any joy.

Mary Magdalene "Ye that kindle a fire, walk in the flame of your fire, and among the brands that ye have kindled. This shall ye have of Mine hand; ye shall lie down in sorrow." The mirth of tabrets ceaseth; the noise of them that rejoice endeth, – our dance is turned to mourning. "This shall ye have of mine hand; ye shall lie down in sorrow."

(There arose a great tempest in the sea)

Mary Magdalene Is Thy wrath against the sea? The voice of Thy thunder is in the heavens! Deep calleth unto deep at the noise of Thy cataracts. I see a ship in the midst of the sea, distressed with waves: and One cometh unto it, walking on the sea! . . . and they that are in the ship, toiling in rowing, are troubled and cry out for fear.

The Apostles (in the ship) It is a spirit!

Jesus Be of good cheer; it is I, be not afraid.

Peter Lord, if it be Thou, bid me come unto Thee upon the waters.

Jesus Come!

The Apostles He walketh upon the waters,

Judas and the Apostles Fearfulness and trembling are come upon him, and an horrible dread hath overwhelmed him.

Peter Lord, save me; I perish!

Mary Magdalene He stretcheth forth His hand

Jesus O Thou of little faith; wherefore didst thou doubt?

Mary Magdalene The wind ceaseth, and they worship Him.

The Apostles Of a truth Thou art the Son of God

Peter, John and Judas The Lord hath his way in the whirlwind and in the storm.

Mary Magdalene Who stilleth the raging of the sea, – Who maketh the storm a calm? Thy providence, O Father, governeth it: for Thou hast made a way in the sea, and a safe path in the waves: shewing that Thou canst save from all danger. Thy face, Lord, will I seek. Thou hast not forsaken them that seek Thee. My soul followeth hard after Thee: Thy right hand upholdeth me.

After the tenor soloist has described the Apostles going out on the lake towards Capernaum, Mary Magdalene in her tower (The Tower of Magdala, a place identified by Longfellow in his poem *The Divine Tragedy*) pleads in her anguish for mercy. Much of the text comes from the Book of Baruch in the Apocrypha, as opposed to more familiar Biblical material. This should have given the scene added weight in its attempt to enter into Mary Magdalene's mind. While much of *The Apostles* could be described as operatic, this intensely moving monologue is particularly so and Elgar creates

66

music aptly suited to the contralto voice. She recalls her past sinful life, a picture which is amplified by the chorus in a rather strangely created 'Fantasy' – a rather unsatisfactory episode which seems out of place and less than convincing in its attempt to relate the temptations of the world from which Mary Magdalene is seeking to escape.

The following, and entirely convincing, orchestral interlude which describes the storm, sets the scene for the Apostles' terror as, in the midst of the tempest, they see Jesus walking toward them on the water. Peter's disastrous attempt to reach his Master is related by the other Apostles. Mary Magdalene, witnessing this and Christ saving Peter from drowning, is convinced of a miracle and thereby converted. Elgar had increasing difficulties with the length of this scene by attempting a response to episodes depicted in Longfellow's poem. The imaginative writing presents events entirely as Mary Magdalene's vision rather than real happenings. The central message of the oratorio – conversion – that this important section sets out to depict is perhaps, therefore, less than convincing. The only unity is not joy at conversion but an unrelieved sorrow on the part of Mary Magdalene throughout.

IN CAESEREA PHILIPPI

Recit. (Tenor) When Jesus came into the parts of Caesarea Philippi, He asked His disciples, saying:

Jesus Whom do men say that I. the Son of Man, am?

The Apostles Some say John the Baptist; some, Elias; and others, Jeremias, or one of the prophets.

Jesus But whom say ye that I am?

Peter Thou art the Christ, the Son of the living God.

Jesus Blessed art thou, Simon Bar-Jona: for flesh and blood hath not revealed it unto thee, but My Father Which is in Heaven. Thou art Peter, – and upon this rock will I build My church; and the gates of Hell shall not prevail against it.

Soli and Chorus Proclaim unto them that dwell on the earth, and unto every nation, and kindred, and tongue, the everlasting Gospel.

Jesus And I will give unto thee the keys of the kingdom of Heaven: and whatsoever thou shalt bind on earth shall be bound in Heaven: and whatsoever thou shalt loose on earth shall be loosed in Heaven.

The scene now moves, without a break, to Caesarea Philippi for Peter's acknowledgement of Christ as God's Son. The words of the tenor soloist are set to music from the previous 'By the Wayside' section. The questions which Christ asks are first answered by the men of the chorus (as Apostles), whose reply echoes the theme from the 'Enigma Variations', but then gloriously by Peter, allowing a fine outburst from the soloists and chorus. Unfortunately, in this rather disjointed section, when something real appears to have been achieved, any anticipated development to take things forward is lost. The scene is foreshortened in an attempt to prolong the only unity, Mary Magdalene's unending sorrow.

One of the more interesting aspects of this brief section is the anticipation of the Lord's Prayer that concludes *The Kingdom.* This occurs when Christ sings 'My Father which is in heaven'. The two works were perhaps still being treated as one in Elgar's mind at this point. Also, the major *leitmotifs* that relate to Peter in the second oratorio are all to be found here.

IN CAPERNAUM

Mary Magdalene Thy face. Lord, will I seek; my soul followeth hard after Thee: help me, desolate woman.

Mary Hearken, O daughter : — when thou art in tribulation, if thou turn to the Lord thy God, and shall be obedient unto His voice, He will not forsake thee. Hearken, O daughter: — Come thou, for there is peace to thee.

Recit. (Tenor) She stood at His feet weeping, and began to wash His feet with tears, and did wipe them with the hairs of her head. And kissed his feet and anointed them with the ointment.

Chorus (Women) This man, if he were a prophet, would have known who and what manner of woman this is that toucheth him: for she is a sinner.

Mary Magdalene Hide not Thy face from me, put not Thy servant away in anger.

Jesus Thy sins are forgiven; thy faith hath saved thee; Go in peace.

Soli and Chorus Turn you to the stronghold, ye prisoners of hope. To the Lord our God belong mercies and forgivenesses, though we have rebelled against Him; turn you to the stronghold, ye prisoners of hope. The fear of the Lord is a crown of wisdom, making peace and perfect health to flourish; both which are the gifts of

God: and it enlargeth their rejoicing that love Him. Turn you to the stronghold, ye prisoners of hope. Thou art the God of the afflicted, Thou art the helper of the oppressed, Thou art the upholder of the weak, Thou art the protector of the forlorn, a Saviour of them that are without hope. Turn you to the stronghold, ye prisoners of hope. Blessed is he who is not fallen from his hope in the Lord. For He will forgive their iniquity, and He will remember their sin no more.

Mary Magdalene continues her search for Christ, this time in Capernaum, where the Virgin Mary gives her comfort in her seemingly unending sorrow. As she reaches Christ, Elgar uses yet another Longfellow suggestion, a paraphrase of Simon the Pharisee's words from St Luke's Gospel, given to the women of the chorus: 'this man, if he were a prophet, would have known who and what manner of woman this is that toucheth him: for she is a sinner'. Elgar observed in a letter to Canon Gorton: 'I have put the words of Simon . . . for the Women (always the hardest on their own sex).'[134] He illustrated this further on one of the original sketches for the music: 'Women mocking (brutes!)'[135], and in his unpublished notes on the libretto he states categorically: 'Simon the Pharisee only thought this: the women of the present day say such things.'[136] Elgar also goes on to explain that he consulted Stainer's oratorio *St Mary Magdalen*, where Saints and theologians including St Augustine, St Ambrose, St Jerome and Dr H. Pusey had been used to justify the view that Mary Magdalene and the penitent woman at Simon the Pharisee's house really were the same person. The inevitable criticism about the not strictly scriptural basis of this variation is, of course, justified on the one hand, but Elgar's very human observations more than explain his thinking here.

The character that actually emerges more strengthened from this scene is Peter, whose smallness of faith is somehow enhanced by his music. Mary Magdalene, whose conversion was crucial to the message of the whole oratorio, remains unconvincing as she is at last forgiven. It was, perhaps, a major miscalculation. Her forgiveness was, in Elgar's original scheme, to have been immediately followed by Judas's betrayal but the length of the work, even at this point, was alarming. Neither had any of his chosen Apostles, with the possible exception of Peter, an opportunity to reveal properly their characters by anything other than fragmentary lines, usually in ensembles. The central character at this point in the oratorio therefore was, at best, a half-hearted heroine whose place in Elgar's original scheme was not a major one.

Part One of *The Apostles* ends with a choral ensemble inserted as an afterthought by Elgar, possibly to add extra weight to the character portrait of Mary Magdalene but, and this seems the more likely explanation, to give the chorus additional music to rehearse. Five months before the first performance – when the Birmingham Festival authorities were anxious for something on which the chorus could work – there was really very little. The music appears to have been written hurriedly and seems, for the most part, unimaginative. The style is more reminiscent of Bach's motet writing or the choral style of Mendelssohn than the Elgar of *The Dream of Gerontius.* The text contains a new Beatitude taken from Ecclesiasticus: 'Blessed is he who is not fallen from his hope in the Lord', which echoes the music of the other Beatitudes Elgar had set earlier. Part One ends quietly, in place of the strong climax which, after such a central event as the only conversion sequence, could perhaps have been expected at this point.

PART II

IV THE BETRAYAL

INTRODUCTION – ORCHESTRA

Part Two of *The Apostles* opens with a slow orchestral introduction in which seven of the principal *leitmotifs* from Part One are repeated. The function of this prelude may be to keep listeners in touch with what has gone before. There is no new material here, although the orchestrations are marginally changed from their original statements. Ernest Newman's description of these forty bars as 'the most unsatisfactory piece of work ever put together by Elgar'[137] and 'where . . . the musical interest diminishes to vanishing point'[138] has some force.

Recit. (Tenor) And it came to pass that He went throughout every city and village, preaching and shewing the glad tidings of the Kingdom of God: and the Twelve were with him; And He began to teach them, that the Son of man must suffer many things and be rejected, and be killed.

Chorus "I will smite the Shepherd, and the sheep of the flock shall be scattered abroad."

Peter Be it far from Thee. Lord, this shall never be unto Thee. Though all men shall be offended because of Thee, yet will I never be offended.

The Apostles Though we should die with Thee, yet will not deny Thee.

Choral Recit. (Tenors and Basses) Then gathered the chief Priests and Pharisees a council, and said: – "What do we? For this Man doeth many miracles." So from that day forth they took counsel that they might put him to death. Then entered Satan into Judas, and he went his way, and communed with the chief Priests and Captains.

Judas What are ye willing to give me, and I will deliver Him unto you?

Chorus (Tenors) And they weighed unto him thirty pieces of silver. Judas then, having received a band of men and officers, cometh with lanterns and torches and weapons.

Judas (Let Him make speed, and hasten His work, that we may see it; He shall bear the glory, and shall sit and rule upon His throne, the great King, – the Lord of the whole earth.)

Whomsoever I shall kiss, that same is He – hold Him fast.

The work now moves into a series of perhaps its finest and most strongly depicted sections, from the Betrayal of Christ to the death of Judas, although the virtue of some scenes is arguably more dramatic than musical.

A tenor recitative, which tells the prophecy by Christ of His death, is preceded with the same three-bar orchestral introduction which opened Part One. The Apostles, including Judas, restate their faith and loyalty in a blending of many of the familiar *leitmotifs*. There is also here an echo of the 'Enigma theme', which is set for Peter to the words 'Be it far from me.' The Priests plot the destruction of Jesus with the help of Judas into whose heart, the text indicates, Satan is said to have entered. This colourful depiction of the action includes a graphic illustration of the 'thirty pieces of silver' in the orchestra (piccolo, flutes, oboes, harps, cymbals, triangle, glockenspiel and organ). From this point Judas becomes the most important of the Apostles in the developing drama: Elgar's music concentrates on illustrating his highly complex character and motives. Canon Gorton in his interpretation of *The Apostles,* which was published by Novello with the approval of the composer, clearly indicates that he was: 'the misguided zealot who would substitute his own plan for Christ's will'.[139] Elgar himself, in his unpublished notes on *The Apostles* libretto, quotes from Latham's *Pastor pastorum* that Judas, 'as maybe the only non-Galilean among the Apostles, wished for patriotic and private reasons to hasten the divine scheme'.[140] The entry in the *Encyclopaedia Britannica* (highlighted by Elgar in his own volume) suggests that Judas had in mind to force Jesus into 'a display of his Messianic power'.[141] From Elgar's other sources it is clear that he supported Daniel Whitby's view, in his *Additional Annotations to the New Testament,* that 'Judas imagined Christ would somehow convey himself out of the soldier's hands and avoid death.'[142] Permission was secured by the composer to reprint the complete Whately lecture from his *Lectures on the Characters of our Lord's Apostles* in his proposed but unpublished commentary on the work. In this lecture (perhaps the prime source of Elgar's thinking) there is an indication that when Christ was condemned without protest and clearly unwilling to save Himself, the full horror of Judas's betrayal overwhelmed the Apostle. Many other explanations have been offered by theologians and authors (including John Masefield) about this interesting character who is so universally reviled.

Judas takes the soldiers to Jesus using words that clearly show his misconception of Christ: 'Let Him make speed and hasten His work. He shall bear the glory and rule upon His throne, the great King – the Lord of the whole earth.' Elgar is closely following Archbishop Whately's view of Judas as a clever, but misguided, man. Elgar is not always at his best here and the many quasi-military *leitmotifs* associated with Roman soldiers and the Temple 'police' could be seen as cliches rather than adding anything to the action.

IN GETHSEMANE

Judas Hail Master!

Jesus Whom seek ye?

The People Jesus of Nazareth.

Jesus I am He: if therefore ye seek Me, let these go their way.

Recit. (Contralto) And they all forsook Him and fled; but Peter followed Him afar off, to see the end.

Choral Recit. (Tenors and Basses) And they that had laid hands on Jesus, led Him away to the High Priest.

During the scene of Jesus's arrest, Elgar ironically quotes a theme from the pastoral episode 'By the wayside' (in Part One of the oratorio). Another interesting, and perhaps puzzling, end to the arrest scene is that the narrative has been given unusually to the contralto soloist before being taken up by the men of the chorus. This is thought to show that Mary Magdalene witnessed the event.

IN THE PALACE OF THE HIGH PRIEST

Servants Thou also wast with Jesus of Nazareth; this man was also with Him

Peter I know not what thou sayest.

Servants Art not thou also one of His disciples?

Peter As thy soul liveth, I am not.

Servants Did we not see thee in the garden with Him? Surely thou art also one of them.

Peter I swear by the Lord, I know not this Man of Whom ye speak.

Recit. (Contralto) Then led they Jesus unto the hail of judgment.

Chorus (Sopranos and Contraltos) And the Lord turned and looked upon Peter, and he went out, and wept bitterly.

Recit. (Contralto) Then Judas, which had betrayed Him, when he saw that He was condemned, repented himself, and brought again the thirty pieces of silver to the chief Priests and Elders.

Any action concerning Christ is, from this point, put well into the background as Elgar concentrates on two main characters, starting with Peter. His denials of Jesus are accompanied by fleeting references to the *leitmotifs* representing his Master and a brief hint of 'The Spirit of the Lord' theme that opened the work. What does, however, stand out in this set piece is the almost unaccompanied female chorus relating how Christ looked at Peter and the remorse that this produced in the Apostle. It is, perhaps, one of the most lovely and impressive short passages in the whole work and recurs in *The Kingdom*.

THE TEMPLE

The Singers (within the Temple) O Lord God, to Whom vengeance belongeth, lift up Thyself, Thou Judge of the earth. O Lord God, to Whom vengeance belongeth, render a reward to the proud. Lord, how long shall the wicked, how long shall the wicked triumph?

Judas My punishment is greater than I can bear.

The Singers How long shall they utter and speak hard things? And all the workers of iniquity boast themselves? They break in pieces Thy people, O Lord, and afflict Thine heritage

Judas Mine iniquity is greater than can be forgiven.

The Priests A voice of trembling, – of fear, why art Thou so grieved in thy mind?

Judas I have sinned in that I have betrayed the innocent blood.

The Priests What is that to us? See thou to that.

Judas I have sinned. – I have betrayed the innocent –

The Priests SELAH!

Recit (Contralto) And he cast down the pieces of silver and departed.

The Singers Lord, how long shall the wicked triumph? Yet they say, The Lord shall not see; He that planted the ear, shall He not hear? He that formed the eye. shall He not see?

Judas (without the Temple) Whither shall I go from Thy Spirit? Or whither shall I flee from Thy presence? If I say, peradventure the darkness shall cover me, then shall my night be turned to day; – yea the darkness is no darkness with Thee, but the night is as clear as the day. Sheol is naked before Thee, and Abaddon hath no covering.

The Singers (within the Temple) Blessed is the man whom Thou chastenest, that Thou mayest give him rest from the days of adversity,

Judas "Rest from the days of adversity," – Never man spake like this Man; He satisfieth the longing soul, and filled the hungry soul with goodness.

The Singers – until the pit be digged for the wicked.

Judas Our life is short and tedious, and in the death of a man there is no remedy; neither was there any man known to have returned from the grave. For we are born at all adventure, and we shall be hereafter as though we had never been; for the breath in our nostrils is as smoke, and a little spark in the moving of our heart, which being extinguished, our body shall be turned into ashes, and our spirit shall vanish as the soft air, and our name shall be forgotten in time, and no man have our work in remembrance; and our life shall pass away as the trace of a cloud, and shall be dispersed as a mist, that is driven away with the beams of the sun and overcome with the heat thereof.

The Singers The Lord knoweth the thoughts of man, that they are vanity.

Judas "The Lord knoweth the thoughts of man," – My hope is like dust that is blown away with the wind; it is not possible to escape Thine hand, – a sudden fear, and not looked for, comes upon me.

The People (remote) Crucify Him!

Judas They gather themselves together and condemn the innocent blood

The People Crucify Him!

Judas Mine end is come, – the measure of my covetousness; over me is spread an heavy night, an image of that darkness which shall afterward receive me; yet am I unto myself more grievous than the darkness.

The Singers (within the Temple) He shall bring upon them their own iniquity.

The time for Elgar's main character (and preoccupation) has now come. This whole desolate night scene, starting with the Betrayal, balances the brilliant opening dawn as Judas, in an obsessive effort to force Christ's hand into a miracle that will convince the world of his power, realises, too late, the enormity of what he has done. Elgar portrays him standing outside the Temple during a service, hearing the singers inside chanting the more implacable terrors of Psalm 94 – a Psalm that asks God to take vengeance against the wicked. He applies the sentiments to himself with a bitter irony and takes his own life.

Judas's repentance is brutally ignored by the Priests, which only increases his anguish. Elgar described the conflict he was trying to portray as: 'a proud sinner [is] swayed by all sorts of feelings.'[143] The character is here wrestling with a unique sense of loneliness which Elgar so successfully gave to Gerontius in a similar state of mind. Not even the small words of comfort that the vengeful Psalm contains can make any impression. Judas is so out of touch with reality that he only picks up the negative words as a mockery of himself. Given the composer's problems with assembling the text of the oratorio, his juxtaposition of Biblical quotations and Psalms is, for the most part, quite masterly. The action is on three continuous planes that the listener experiences simultaneously, knowing that neither Judas nor the singers within the Temple can possibly be aware of each other. In the third plane, the bass parts of the orchestra outline, to a large extent, the very heartbeats of Judas as he is carried inexorably towards his own self-destruction.

This music is amongst the finest and most intense that Elgar ever wrote. He recalls themes from appropriate sections of the oratorio in a continued increase of tension where a distraught and defeated Judas reflects on the goodness of Christ. By using the telling *leitmotif* from the Beatitudes in Section Two of the oratorio, Judas is shown as realising the irreversible mistake he has made. This is further illustrated by him using and developing snatches of the phrases chanted by the Temple singers. There are some problems however, such as Elgar's, perhaps inappropriate, use of material from *The Light of Life* when Judas is craving darkness and death. Elgar was less adept than some other composers, such as Wagner, at depicting irony in his music.

Elgar could never satisfactorily explain the derivation of the single word 'SELAH!' (flashed out by the men of the chorus imitating the Priests). It is apparently a traditional Jewish expression that defies translation. The word appears in the Psalms as an occasional directive about singing or ceremonial. Elgar seems to have used it as a rude dismissal. An example of this appears in a letter: 'There are fine rows going on over the first performance [of the Violin Concerto] and I am desperately annoyed over several things: selah!'[144] Yet again, in a letter to Troyte Griffith he gives a whole paragraph to the single word 'SELAH!'. [145]

When the distant cries of the chorus 'Crucify Him' become overwhelming, Judas, filled with total horror, kills himself. This is represented in the orchestra, culminating with a rapid restatement of the main theme for Christ himself. Elgar obviously wished the listener to know that Judas's last thoughts were of the man he had betrayed. He described this short orchestral episode as one where: 'a man of action . . . staggers about in a ghastly way.'[146] An interesting note appears in some of Elgar's papers relating to the cry of 'Crucify Him'. He had been given, at Christmas 1902, all eight volumes of Wagner's *Prose Works* translated by W. A. Ellis. Elgar's pencilled comment: 'Wagner'[147] on a sketch titled: 'Judas. Crucify Him'[148] may refer to a similar scene in the final volume, *Jesus of Nazareth*, of the Wagner set.

Judas, although strictly speaking a subsidiary character, remains the central figure of this scene and it is *his* tragedy, not Christ's, which remains fixed in the listener's mind. He is an entirely convincing human figure. Anyone encountering this broken man outside the Temple listening to the Psalm of vengeance from within has a rare glimpse of ultimate despair. But it should also be remembered that the despair was also Elgar's own as he set the words (from the *Book of Wisdom*): 'Our name shall be forgotten in time, and no man shall have our work in remembrance, and our life shall pass away as the trace of a cloud, and shall be dispersed as a mist, that is driven away with the beams of the sun, and overcome with the heat thereof.' This was Elgar's fear to the end of his life. As the composer had breathed life into the character of Gerontius and made the audience care, so Judas is a compelling figure from exactly the same mould – worldly, sinful and about to receive judgement. This unusual treatment of a character universally misunderstood by history could have been guided by Elgar's lack of real insight into wickedness, but it is far more likely that, given the care with which the text is assembled and the music written, Elgar knew that he had got the portrait right. Judas's suicide commands sympathy and not condemnation. There is no mysticism here, only dramatic reality, as Elgar intended.

V GOLGOTHA

(Muted Strings)
["Eli, Eli, lama sabachthani?"]

Chorus Truly this was the Son of God.

Mary The sword hath pierced through mine own soul.

Mary and John Thou hast trodden the winepress alone, and of Thy people there was none with Thee. They shall look upon Him Whom they have pierced, and they shall mourn for Him, as one mourneth for his only son. And shall be in bitterness for Him, as one that is in bitterness for his firstborn.

Mary The sword hath pierced through mine own soul.

In *The Apostles* the Crucifixion is hardly shown and simply alluded to by seven adagio bars of orchestral music with the last of Christ's words from the Cross: 'Eli, Eli, lama sabachtani?' ('My God, My God, why hast Thou forsaken me?'), printed over them. Elgar told Canon Gorton: 'I chose this rather than either of the other "last words" because it permits me to use much of the rest of the Ps [22] in the Ascension chorus.'[149] Interestingly, when this music reaches its climax, Elgar determined to use the chord which introduced the Angel of the Agony in *The Dream of Gerontius*. The dissonance does not, perhaps, have quite the same impact, although the idea remains. In a letter to Hamilton Harty, Elgar makes it clear that he had something larger in mind to depict the earthquake at Christ's death. All that appears is a single, rather nondescript bar of music. He told Harty: 'in a fit of laziness, I suppose, I wrote one bar — it should have been <u>four</u>: you will see the <u>great cresc</u> [endo] and the *ff* tearing of the 3 Trumpets.'[150] Was it laziness or an unwillingness to set this momentous event? Did Elgar wish to direct attention back to the Apostles, whose story he was really trying to tell, by passing so quickly over this major event and the Resurrection that followed? Were these such painful events that he could not bring himself to set them? It is true to say that Elgar would not have seriously attempted the vision of the Soul going before God in *The Dream of Gerontius* without continual pressure from August Jaeger. The crucial battle for Britain was similarly avoided in *Caractacus*. Might listeners be entitled to assume that without external pressure Elgar actually felt unequal to setting the death of Christ or His Resurrection?

Grief is, however, evident both from the awestruck entry of the chorus (whose 'Truly, this was the Son of God' is more than a match for the familiar setting by J. S. Bach in the *St Matthew Passion*) to the halting dialogue between the Virgin Mary and the Apostle John. There are also some references here to the Angel Gabriel's solo from the start of Part One.

VI AT THE SEPULCHRE

Recit. (Contralto) And very early in the morning they came unto the sepulchre at the rising of the sun; and they entered in, and found not the body of the Lord Jesus.

The Watchers (on the Temple roof) The face of all the East is now ablaze with light; the Dawn reacheth even unto Hebron!

Chorus (Angels) (Sopranos and Contraltos) Alleluia!

Why seek ye the living among the dead? He is not here, but is risen. Behold the place where they laid Him. Go, tell His disciples and Peter that He goeth before you into Galilee: there shall ye see Him, as he said unto you.

Alleluia!

As dawn breaks on the third day, and with the tomb empty, the contralto starts a brief retelling of the Resurrection story. Elgar takes his lead in this short section from Longfellow's poem *The Two*

Marys, and sets the narrative almost entirely for female voices. Listeners are briefly reminded of the dawn from Part One as the watchers on the Temple roof again take up the morning Psalm to the sound of the shofar. But it is out of this fragmentary section that the first notes of the Angels' 'Alleluias' (a reflection of Elgar's other Angel who sings similar sublime 'Alleluias' in *The Dream of Gerontius*) that will give an entirely new radiance to the work and be sustained to the very end, are heard. This first statement (for unaccompanied female voices in four parts) is utterly simple. Elgar, not always at his best in really simple music, here works this brief episode with a kind of magical wonder.

VII   THE ASCENSION

The Apostles We trusted that it had been He which should have redeemed Israel.

Jesus Peace be unto you. Behold, I send the promise of My Father upon you: but tarry ye in the city of Jerusalem, until ye be endued with power from on high.

The Apostles Lord, wilt Thou at this time restore again the kingdom to Israel?

Jesus It is not for you to know the times or the seasons, which the Father hath put in His own power. But ye shall receive power, when the Holy Ghost is come upon you. Go ye therefore, and teach all nations, baptizing them in the name of the Father, and of the Son, and of the Holy Ghost; and, lo, I am with you alway, even unto the end of the world.

Recit. (Contralto) And when He had spoken these things – while He blessed them – He was taken up; and a cloud received Him out of their sight; and they looked steadfastly toward Heaven.

The Apostles Give us one heart, and one way: in Thy light shall we see light; Thou wilt shew us the path of life.

Mystic Chorus (In Heaven) Alleluia!

Mary, Mary Magdalene, John and Peter Give us one heart, and one way.

Mary My soul doth magnify the Lord: and my spirit hath rejoiced in God my Saviour.

79

(*Mary Magdalene*) Thou drewest near in the day that I called upon Thee: Thou saidst, Fear not.

Peter For He hath not despised nor abhorred the affliction of the afflicted; neither hath He hid His face from him;

The Apostles and the Holy Women but when he cried unto Him, He heard.

Mystic Chorus Alleluia!

"*Holy Father, keep through Thine own name those whom Thou hast given Me, that they may be one, as We are.*"

The Apostles and the Holy Women All the ends of the world shall remember and turn unto the Lord: and all the kindreds of the nations shall worship before Thee, for the Kingdom is the Lord's: and He is the Governor among the nations.

Mystic Chorus Alleluia!

"*I have done Thy commandment. I have finished the work which Thou gavest me to do: I have laid down My life for the sheep.*"

The Apostles "In the world shall ye have tribulation: but be of good cheer: I have overcome the world."

Mystic Chorus "What are these wounds in Thine hands?" 'Those with which I was wounded in the house of My friends.'

They platted a crown of thorns, and put it about His head. – they mocked Him, – they spat upon Him, – they smote Him with a reed, – they crucified Him.

Alleluia!

The Apostles and the Holy Women They shall come, and shall declare His righteousness unto a people that shall be born, that He hath done this.

Mystic Chorus "Now I am no more in the world, but these are in the world, and I come to Thee."

The Apostles and the Holy Women The kingdom is the Lord's: and He is the Governor among the nations.

Mystic Chorus From henceforth shall the Son of man be seated at the right hand of the power of God.

Mary, Mary Magdalene, John and Peter In His love and in His pity He redeemed them.

Tutti Alleluia!

The final section contains the longest dramatic solo for Christ in the whole work. This music uses many of the main *leitmotifs,* and the text deals with Christ's promise to the Apostles that they will receive power from the Holy Ghost – dramatically setting the scene for *The Kingdom* that was to follow. After the contralto soloist has detailed the Ascension, the chorus becomes the mystic chorus (in Heaven) responding to the pleas of the Apostles and the two Marys left on earth. Heaven and earth are at last combined in a grand and comprehensive design. The heavenly choir take up the words of Christ and detail the events of the Crucifixion, punctuated with 'Alleluias', as the work builds to a mighty restatement of the main Prayer theme that has appeared at all the major climaxes in *The Apostles.* The music then gradually recedes with earthly and heavenly 'Alleluias' as the two Marys, Peter and John sing of the world's redemption through the death and Resurrection of Christ, to music taken directly from the first solo entry in *The Dream of Gerontius* – 'And Thou art Calling Me'. Elgar's conscious use of this quotation here is puzzling. It is not elaborated on but momentarily stands out from the whole before disappearing just as quickly.

While much of the text Elgar chooses throughout *The Apostles* to illustrate his thinking is appropriate, this final section contains a strange quotation, the use of which has never been satisfactorily explained. Longdon Marsh and the nearby church at Queenhill provided much of the inspiration for the Ascension scene, and it was the chance purchase of a small pamphlet on sale in the church which produced the words, from the Book of Zachariah: 'What are these wounds in Thy hands?' This line was perfectly suited to Elgar's purpose but he then adds a line from Ezekiel: 'Those with which I was wounded in the house of my friends' as a rather unusual response. There is no evidence to suggest that he received anything but support from his friends during the crisis over *The Apostles* and the quotation does not fit easily with the ideas apparent in the dedication of the 'Enigma Variations' – 'to my friends pictured within'.

CHAPTER TWELVE

THE PUBLISHED SCORES OF
'THE APOSTLES'

The final version of the full orchestral score approved by Elgar was not available from Novello & Co. until April 1904 following rehearsals in Birmingham for the work's second British performance. In a letter to Jaeger, the composer commented that there was '. . . only one error in the score which is also very good considering the complications.'[151] Research for the most recent edition shows, however, that while Elgar underestimated the errors (342 corrections were required), his overall assessment of Novello's work on the final score was, at that point, valid.

Elgar had given Novello the 'final authority to print the full orchestral score'[152] in late February 1904. This was the end of a long process that started with translating the sketches of the oratorio into a vocal score required for the commencement of choral rehearsals in Birmingham on 11 July 1903. The vocal score would also be used by Elgar when the soloists were auditioned and then for them to study in preparation for the premiere. A complete realisation of the vocal score would also determine the final shape of the work for orchestration as a composite whole, but the process was not to be an easy one for any of those involved.

With the first section sent to the publishers in January 1903, Elgar continued composition of the oratorio at the same time as proof-reading the material engraved by Novello & Co. This haphazard process hindered both composition and the correcting of proofs to the extent that when the composer needed to try over the third section, 'By the Sea of Galilee', with his chosen soloist Muriel Foster – the future Mary Magdalene – in April 1903, the proofs were not ready. In May, while considering the question of who should sing the part of Judas, Elgar was angry that proofs of the music for the 'Betrayal Scene' should have been put back for the insertion of the new final chorus, 'Turn ye to the Stronghold', hurriedly produced to complete Part One. The Festival authorities were becoming concerned that the vocal score supplied, already contained too little for the chorus to rehearse. The question of finding an adequate Judas was later to become the potential pretext Elgar used with his publishers for revising and reducing the final sections of the oratorio. He also changed his mind several times about using the designation 'Saint' for some of the characters and how the Virgin Mary should be named. But by July Part One was ready for the chorus rehearsals and Part Two – completed by Elgar on 24 June – followed in August. Further alterations, such as the holding back of a page on 4 August for the insertion of a *leitmotif*, while not changing the chorus music but necessitating the rewriting of several bars in the accompaniment, and again on 10 August a similar change to another page, created major difficulties at the publishers.

As was usual with Elgar's printed vocal scores, the first edition of *The Apostles* included some indications of the subsequent orchestration, particularly the references to the shofar, a Jewish Temple instrument. It is also clear from the vocal score proofs that at one time it was Elgar's

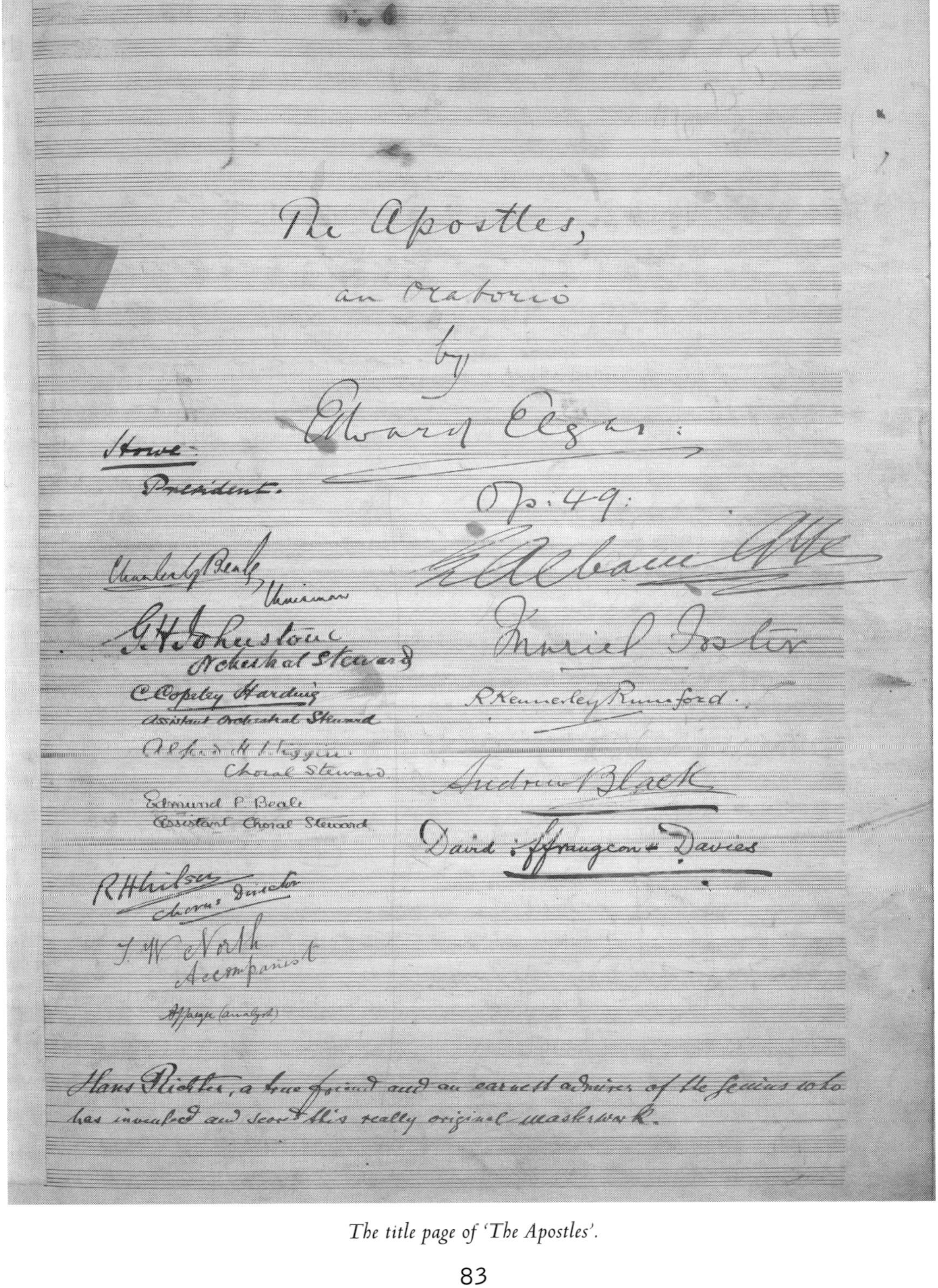

The title page of 'The Apostles'.

intention to include many more 'instrumental cues' than finally appeared in the published edition.

Just five days after finishing the vocal score Elgar began to orchestrate the oratorio, but the process with this was just as haphazard as with all his previous work. Completed sections would be sent to William Dodd in Kew – who was making the orchestral parts – via Novello. The first 48 pages were received on 10 July with Elgar's instructions that 'generous cues' should be included in the parts and that, before printing, the composer should check all the parts personally against his own manuscript full orchestral score. This was, of course, a time-consuming process but from page 50 of full orchestral score Elgar was able to make use of the vocal score proofs arriving almost daily from the publishers. On these he indicated in pencil the page numbers for the orchestral score as well as sketching out a good deal of the orchestration. 'By the Wayside' was scored in full by 16 July and the rest of Part One finished at the home of his friend Alfred Rodewald in Betws-y-Coed, where the Elgars were staying, between 3 and 31 July. The string parts were collated concurrently with the scoring of Part Two which was completed at Malvern Wells on 17 August. Elgar wrote to Jaeger: 'By this post comes some revised string parts & corresponding portions of the score. /& two sections completing the work. Alleluia!'[153]

As orchestral rehearsals for *The Apostles* were scheduled for Belle Vue, Manchester, to start on 5 October, the orchestral parts had to be ready by then. The string parts were being engraved not by William Dodd in London but by F. M. Geidel in Leipzig because of his specialist knowledge. This, of course, produced further delays that hindered complete work on correction of the parts by Elgar at Novello or his home in Malvern Wells where he was greatly assisted by John Austin, Ivor Atkins and sometimes Alice Elgar. The composer's way of checking the parts was to play through them on the violin accompanied on the piano. But as delays in supplying the engraved parts increased during the second half of September, Elgar made repeated requests for the string parts from Leipzig – 'Horns and transposing things at least'[154] – from Dodd who assured the publishers that he would be finished by the end of the month. On 30 September Elgar was near to collapse and plagued with eye trouble. When they did arrive, the horn and clarinet parts failed to include Elgar's special dynamic markings – *ritardando, accelerando* and *largamente* – but there was no time for correction. Many superfluous indications in these parts also had to be left in. Finally, on 1 October, Geidel sent a telegram from Leipzig to say that the string parts had been dispatched direct to Manchester. The day before the orchestral rehearsal Alice Elgar noted in her diary that her husband and John Austin were 'still working on the band parts.'[155]

By 20 October, almost a week after the premiere, Elgar had written to Jaeger about the printing of the complete (corrected) orchestral parts and the full orchestral score. By early November the first proofs, engraved by Geidel, were acknowledged but proof-reading them was interrupted by the death of Alfred Rodewald on 9 November. This affected Elgar to the extent that he asked for the reading to be dealt with by Novello & Co.: 'Pointer and Brooke can do it all for the present & perhaps I can see to a revise later'.[156]

Elgar, with his wife, left for Italy on 25 November. By this time Elgar was receiving proofs again and he wrote to Jaeger on 5 December: 'By this post, proof corrected; there seem to be many errors not marked: tell Pointer & Co. I have my eye on them'.[157] Corrections continued in Italy, and on 3 February 1904, soon after the Elgars return to England and on the day they dined with the King, Jaeger brought the final score of *The Apostles* to the hotel.

In Italy, with the process almost at an end, Elgar had written a brief letter of thanks to his helpers at Novello & Co. It was in Italian, addressed to 'Ai Signori l'Occidente, Cacciatore, Cane da fermo et Ruscello [West, Jaeger, Pointer, Brooke]' and signed 'Hochachtungavoli/EDUARDO ELGARO'.[158]

CHAPTER THIRTEEN

'THE KINGDOM' op. 51
IN MORE DETAIL

For *The Kingdom*, Elgar did not specify such a large orchestra as that used in *The Apostles*. Once again the woodwind is augmented by a bass clarinet and double bassoon but the percussion requirements are reduced to a large gong, cymbals and a side drum, plus the usual timpani. The organ retains an important part, independent of doubling the chorus. Unlike in *The Apostles* the second harp is not optional.

Due to revisions in the scale of the work there are parts for only four soloists:

The Blessed Virgin	Soprano
Mary Magdalene	Contralto
St John	Tenor
St Peter	Bass

Elgar's use of the large chorus — soprano, alto, tenor and bass — does not have the complexity of *The Apostles* and is only briefly divided into chorus and semi-chorus, although sometimes split into six or more parts. Throughout the work the chorus mainly take the part of 'the other Disciples' (that is the group apart from Elgar's central characters of Peter and John) but briefly assume less distinct and more impersonal roles.

When Elgar belatedly started work on *The Kingdom* he still intended the oratorio to take the Apostles story forward to the establishment of the Christian Church at Antioch. What eventually emerged were only the scenes planned for Part One of the new work, concluding with the 'Breaking of Bread' and the Lord's Prayer. The action therefore never moves from Jerusalem. It is clear that Elgar had some libretto written for the scenes in his proposed Part Two and the most fully developed is that of Simon of Gitta (who challenged Peter for supremacy in the establishment of the Church). He was the sorcerer from Samaria and Helen of Tyre's lover according to Elgar's source – Acts 8. Simon is shown as trying to purchase from Peter the power to give the Holy Spirit and his name is also the source of the word 'simony' (the buying or selling of ecclesiastical privileges). It is clear that this character was destined to replace Judas as antagonist in Elgar's scheme. The evil would culminate in the Antichrist of *The Last Judgement*. Again Elgar researched widely, from the *Encyclopaedia Britannica* to Longfellow's 'Simon Magus and Helen of Tyre' in *The Divine Tragedy* via Hippolytus (an early church writer). This produced the legend of a sorcerer who was capable of materialising anywhere he chose. The text that would have opened the scene, 'In Samaria' (where Simon Magus was born), concerns Jacob's Well and the Women of Samaria referred to in John 4. The latter is of interest in that Elgar had marked the passages in his *Red Letter New Testament* with a margin note 'Simon Magus must have known all this.'[159] There follows a chorus

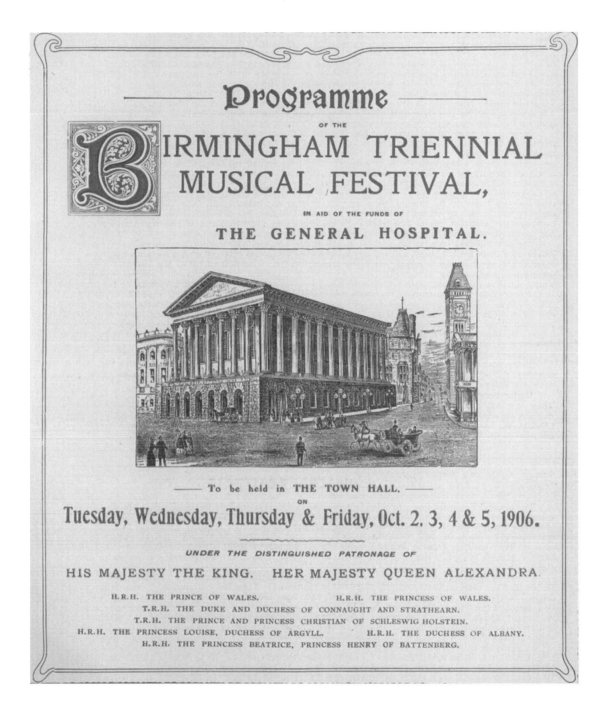

The 1906 Birmingham Triennial Festival Programme Book

PROGRAMME.

WEDNESDAY MORNING, OCTOBER 3RD, 1906.

Part 1.

ORATORIO - - - - "THE KINGDOM" (Op. 51) - - Edward Elgar.

First time of Performance.

(CONDUCTED BY THE COMPOSER.)

THE BLESSED VIRGIN ...	Miss AGNES NICHOLLS.
MARY MAGDALENE ...	Miss MURIEL FOSTER.
ST. JOHN ...	Mr. JOHN COATES.
ST. PETER ...	Mr. WILLIAM HIGLEY.

JERUSALEM.

PRELUDE (Orchestra).

I.—IN THE UPPER ROOM.

CHORUS (The Disciples and the Holy Women) ... ... Seek first the Kingdom.
RECIT. (Peter) ... ... Peace be multiplied unto you.
CHORUS (The Disciples and the Holy Women) ... } Remember the words of the Lord Jesus.
RECIT. (Peter) ... ... He took bread.
CHORUS (The Disciples and the Holy Women) ... The true Vine.
TUTTI ... ... Let them give thanks whom the Lord hath redeemed.

RECIT. (Peter) ... ... Men and brethren.
CHORUS (The Disciples and the Holy Women) ... ... Let his habitation be desolate.
RECIT. (Peter) ... ... Wherefore of these men which have companied with us.
CHORUS (The Disciples) ... { Thou, Lord, Which knowest the hearts of all men. They gave forth their lots.
SOLI ... ... The Lord hath chosen.

CHORUS ... ... O ye priests !

II.—AT THE BEAUTIFUL GATE.

THE MORN OF PENTECOST.

SOLO (Mary) ... ... The singers are before the altar; they make sweet melody.
SOLO (Mary Magdalene) ... This man, lame from his mother's womb.
SOLO (Mary) ... ... The blind and the lame came to Jesus.
SOLO (Mary Magdalene) ... The service of the Lord is prepared.

III.—PENTECOST.

IN THE UPPER ROOM.

RECIT., TENOR ... ... And when the day of Pentecost was fully come.
CHORUS (The Disciples) ... When the great Lord will.
MYSTIC CHORUS (Soprano and Contralto) ... ... The Spirit of the Lord shall rest upon them.
SOLO (John) ... ... When the Comforter is come.
SOLO (Peter) ... ... And speak as moved by the Holy Spirit.
MYSTIC CHORUS ... ... I will pour forth of My Spirit.

RECIT., CONTRALTO ... ... And suddenly there came from heaven a sound.
CHORUS (The Disciples) ... He Who walketh upon the wings of the wind.
MYSTIC CHORUS ... ... (The Lord put forth His hand.)
RECIT., CONTRALTO ... ... And there were dwelling at Jerusalem.

IN SOLOMON'S PORCH.

CHORUS (The People) ... Behold, are not all these.
SOLO (John) ... ... He, Who walketh upon the wings of the wind.
CHORUS (The People) ... What meaneth this?
SOLO (Peter) ... ... He, Whose ministers are flaming fire.
CHORUS (The People) ... With stammering lips.
RECIT. (Peter) ... ... "I have prayed for thee, that thy faith fail not."
SOLO ... ... Ye men of Judæa.
CHORUS (The People) ... (His blood be on us.)
SOLO, CONTRALTO ... ... (Daughters of Jerusalem.)
CHORUS (The People) ... Men and brethren, what shall we do?
SOLO (Peter) ... ... Repent, and be baptized.
CHORUS (The People) ... In the Name of Jesus Christ.
TUTTI (SOLI AND CHORUS) ... The First-Fruits.

IV.—THE SIGN OF HEALING.

AT THE BEAUTIFUL GATE.

RECIT., CONTRALTO ... ... Then they that gladly received his word.
RECIT., CONTRALTO ... ... The man that was lame, at the Beautiful Gate.
SOLO (Peter) ... ... Look on us.
CHORUS (The People) ... This is he which sat for alms.
SOLO (Peter) ... ... Ye men of Israel.
SOLO (John) ... ... Unto you that fear His Name.
DUET (Peter and John) ... Turn ye again, that your sins may be blotted out.

THE ARREST.

RECIT., CONTRALTO ... ... And as they spake.
RECIT., CONTRALTO ... ... It was now eventide.
Orchestra.
SOLO (Mary) ... ... The sun goeth down.

V.—THE UPPER ROOM.

IN FELLOWSHIP.

CHORUS (The Disciples and the Holy Women) ... ... The voice of joy.
RECIT. (John) ... ... The rulers asked.
CHORUS (The Disciples and the Holy Women) ... ... In none other is there salvation.
RECIT. (Peter) ... ... And when they took knowledge of us.
RECIT. (John) ... ... Finding nothing how they might punish us.
CHORUS (The Disciples and the Holy Women) ... } Lord, Thou didst make the heaven.

THE BREAKING OF BREAD.

CHORUS (The Disciples and the Holy Women) ... ... Thou, Almighty Lord.
RECIT. (Peter) ... ... If any is holy.
CHORUS (The Disciples) ... Let him come.
RECIT. (John) ... ... Give thanks; first for the Cup.
CHORUS (The Disciples and the Holy Women) ... We thank Thee.
TUTTI ... ... As this Broken Bread was grain scattered upon the mountains.

THE PRAYERS.

TUTTI ... ... OUR FATHER.
SOLO (John) ... ... Ye have received.
TUTTI ... ... Thou, O Lord, art our Father, our Redeemer.

Part 2.

MOTET (Double Chorus) - - "Sing ye to the Lord" - - - - - J. S. Bach.

SYMPHONY No. 1, in C minor - - - - - - - - - - - Brahms.

Morning Programme, 3 October 1906

'With joy shall ye draw water out of the wells of salvation' based on Isaiah 12. Other libretto notes indicate that the Samarian scene was to be prepared for by Simon Magus accompanying the Holy Women at Solomon's Porch in Scene II of *The Kingdom*. There was also to be a significant sceptical part for the character after the descent of the Holy Spirit.

Musical sketches for the Simon scenes show a difference of approach from the generally predictable tone of *The Kingdom* as a whole. It is harsh and chromatic, reflecting the Judas ideas in *The Apostles*. His warped character finds expression in phrases like: 'To me they all gave heed, from the least to the greatest, saying: "This man is the power of God which is called great".'[160] Much of the material is set to familiar *leitmotifs*, although Simon Magus does have several new themes of his own scattered throughout the sketches.

Other projected scenes included the conversion of the Centurion Cornelius (the first Gentile convert); the conversion of many in Antioch; the martyrdom of Stephen – 'Stone him to death, I give my voice against him!' was part of the text which Elgar adapted from Acts 6:26; the conversion of Saul, and the story of Ananias and Sapphira.

The scenes at Antioch were particularly attractive. As Christ had given Peter a new name, Christ's followers were named 'Christians' there for the first time. Elgar queried whether any connection could be made between these events in a practical (not contrived) way and made pages of libretto notes based on the many Bible concordance entries about the name 'Christians.'[161] There was a query about a possible chariot race based on a note quoting Isaiah: 'their land is full of horses, neither is there any end of their chariots.' This idea is further developed in Elgar's notes on the *Book of Nahum*: 'the noise of the rattling of the wheels and the pransing [sic] horses, and of the jumping chariots'. Capel-Cure was less than enthusiastic: 'no chance I fear of finding anything for a chariot race wh. was only for a short time adopted after Hellenizing contacts before the patriotic swing under the Maccabees'.[162] Strangely, as an alternative, Capel-Cure suggested the very risky story from Ezekiel about the 'appalling whoredoms' of Aholah and Aholibah!'[163] Was Antioch to be a 'joyous city, whose antiquity is of ancient days'?[164] Elgar did, however, note that the city was founded only in 300 BC. He next considered the pleasure ground of Daphne near Antioch for setting a text from Wisdom 17 originally written into the Beatitudes scene in *The Apostles*: 'a melodious noise of birds among the spreading branches, [or a pleasing fall of water running violently]'[165] – the last words were deleted from the draft. The musical sketches associated with Antioch are mainly from discarded Mary Magdalene material in *The Apostles*.

At the outset there seemed more time for Elgar to consider this, the central oratorio of the projected trilogy, but once again, with no proper libretto, composition became more and more difficult. The only partial advantage for him was that some material had already been written but unused in *The Apostles*.

With less drama and no real character portraits, *The Kingdom* is characterised by gentle reflection on events in an atmosphere of great happiness and warmth. But this in itself could be seen as a weakness. If listeners are to assume that Peter has now become the most important character – the text and several important solos underline this – why does he never achieve any real status musically? Perhaps the answer lies in the fact that very little new music is given to him and his words are continually set to familiar themes, from *The Apostles* or the Prelude to *The Kingdom,* without further proper development, at a time when it is clear that Peter has come a long way since his failure by the denial of Christ. It is, perhaps, difficult to be seen as a commanding figure if you are continually dressed in old clothes.

The Kingdom consists of a Prelude and five scenes. Within each of these sections there are a few almost unrelated solos and choruses but most of this oratorio is based on ensembles that are created from seamless weaving of soloists, chorus and orchestra.

The basic text relies mainly on The Acts of the Apostles amplified by extra references: —

I   IN THE UPPER ROOM - Acts 1; St Matthew 5:14; St John 14:6; 15:1; St Mark 14:22

II   AT THE BEAUTIFUL GATE - Acts 3:2

III   PENTECOST - Acts 2

IV   THE SIGN OF HEALING - Acts 2:41; 3:2,6,9,10,12; 4:1

V   THE UPPER ROOM - Acts 4:7 onwards

JERUSALEM

PRELUDE

The broad sweep of the orchestral Prelude produces the most extended and complete example of symphonic writing in either *The Apostles* or *The Kingdom.* Of Elgar's three major religious choral works, the opening of *The Kingdom* is perhaps the most exciting and appears to be a musical release akin to that of Wagner when starting Act Three of *Siegfried.* It is completely uninhibited and does not over-reinforce the themes used by continual repetition, but develops them in a highly original way as links are made between the two oratorios of the trilogy. Many of the principal themes are associated with Peter to indicate that he has now become the leader of the remaining Apostles. The central section, marked *Andante dolce e solenne,* is reminiscent of Elgar's Second Symphony, the sketches of which date from the same time as he began serious work on *The Kingdom.* It is actually a fairly elaborate development of the Gregorian Antiphon *O sacrum convivium* from which much of *The Apostles* thematic material is derived.

In this highly original Prelude the progression from fervour to solid resolution via frenzy and loneliness could be seen as indicating the vigour with which the Apostles start their mission; Peter's succession to the leadership, but his inner doubts, prompted by the denial of his Master, leading to a feeling of renewed mission through Christ's forgiveness.

I   THE UPPER ROOM

The Disciples and the Holy Women Seek first the Kingdom of God, and His righteousness.

Peter Peace be multiplied unto you.

The Disciples and the Holy Women Peace; peace be unto thee, and peace be to thine helpers.

Peter "Where two or three are gathered together in My Name, there am I in the midst of them."

Mary, Mary Magdalene, John and Peter Remember the words of the Lord Jesus, —

The Disciples and the Holy Women Jesus, the Holy One.

John "Surely they are my people":

The Disciples and the Holy Women so He was their Saviour;

Mary For while all things were in quiet silence, and that night was in the midst of her swift course, Thine almighty Word leaped down from Heaven out of Thy royal throne.

The Disciples and the Holy Women The Light of the world

Mary Magdalene The Dayspring from on high hath visited us, to guide our feet into the way of peace.

The Disciples and the Holy Women The Way, the Truth, and the Life.

John Did not their heart burn within them, while he talked with them by the way?

Peter He took bread, and blessed it, and brake, and gave it to us.

The Disciples and the Holy Women The true Vine; the Bread of Life.

All Let them give thanks whom the Lord hath redeemed; He remembered His holy promise. In the concord of bretheren, in the love of neighbours. O praise the Name of the Lord our God. The true Vine, the Bread of Life: He brake, and gave it to us. Praise the Name of our God. That hath dealt wondrously with us. Amen.

Peter Men and bretheren: it was needful that the scripture should be fulfilled, which the Holy Ghost spake before by the mouth of David concerning Judas, who was guide to them that took Jesus: for he was numbered among us, and had obtained part of this ministry.

The Disciples and the Holy Women "Let his habitation be desolate, and let no man dwell therein, and his office let another take."

Peter Wherefore of these men which have companied with us all the time that the Lord Jesus went in and out among us, must one be ordained to be witness with us of His resurrection.

Peter, John and the Disciples Thou, Lord, Which knowest the hearts of all men, shew of these two the one whom Thou hast chosen, to take the place in this ministry and apostleship.

Choral recit. They gave forth their lots: (The lot is cast; but the whole disposing thereof is of the Lord), and the lot fell upon Matthias; and he was numbered with the eleven Apostles.

John, Peter, Mary, Mary Magdalene, the Disciples and the Holy Women The Lord hath chosen you to stand before Him to serve Him; you shall be named the Priest of the Lord.

Chorus O ye priests! Seemeth it but a small thing that God hath separated you to bring you near to Himself, to stand before the congregation to minister unto them? For it is not ye that speak, but the spirit of your Father which speaketh in you: the Lord hath chosen you; ye are the messengers of the Lord of hosts. It is not ye that speak, but the spirit of your Father Which speaketh in you. O ye priests! This commandment is for you.

The Upper Room, in Jerusalem, is where the Apostles and the Holy Women have returned after Christ's Ascension. They are meeting to remember, pray and give thanks. John's brief reference to The Journey to Emmaus – 'Did not their hearts burn within them, as He talked with them by the way' – is taken from a sketch of this scene destined for, but unused in, *The Apostles*. The whole Emmaus episode was to have been treated quite elaborately in the earlier oratorio. Peter takes charge by greeting the assembly to an orchestral accompaniment based on the antiphon *O sacrum convivium*. This theme appears throughout *The Kingdom* to indicate the abiding spiritual presence of Christ with his people. Scattered *leitmotifs* from *The Apostles* appear throughout this section, culminating in an 'Amen'. For a work that started out with such energy, the seemingly tired repetition of old material at such an early stage perhaps underlines the difficulty which Elgar was already experiencing in continuing. This is typical of both *The Apostles* and *The Kingdom*, where recourse to the more certain past often replaces a very uncertain future in the composer's thinking.

Peter, with new authority, addresses the group about the necessity of choosing a replacement for Judas. The style of this free recitative – by turns declamatory and then lyrical – had become typical of Elgar. Once again, and despite the obvious renewed enthusiasm with which Elgar approached this section, there is a perhaps understandable reliance on *leitmotifs* from *The Apostles* as Peter's ideas range further. In a graphic musical illustration the Disciples make their choice by casting lots, despite an obvious tension at the suspense reflected in varied cross-rhythms. When Matthias is selected the fear evaporates in an energetic chorus about future vocation. Canon Gorton in his interpretation of the libretto explained that: 'the message the composer would have us to understand echoes down through the ages. The lot, on whomsoever it may fall, be he preacher, teacher, administrator or artist, is from the Lord.'[166] It may therefore be possible for the listener to approach *The Kingdom* as an allegory of both creative and religious inspiration. August Jaeger, who was by this time very ill, in putting together his 'Analytical and Descriptive Notes' on *The Kingdom*, could not accept the necessity for the 'choice by lot' section. This doubt received short shrift from Alice Elgar, who wrote back:

> 'It is curious that that Chorus did not fire you, it works up all who have heard it to a great pitch of excitement – & I think you might have given E. some credit for his really fine literary taste & poetic feeling in his selection of words . . . so instead of "Matthias" meaning nothing to us, it is the type of Everything wh. can still infuse heroism, self sacrifice & great thoughts into all those who are not dead to such things.'[167]

This is one of the few occasions when Elgar uses his chorus in a more impersonal way. The section ends in calm mood, the motive for which has some affinity with reflective episodes in the Passions of J. S. Bach. The method is very different, though, and the assignment to solo voices or via the medium of a congregational chorale is here replaced by the imaginative use of full chorus and orchestra. Therefore the apparently disproportionate use of forces for such a simple end actually works.

Yet despite all the effort of such a big ensemble to symbolise the choosing of a new Apostle and the implied promise for the future, despite the re-assembly of powerful themes from *The Apostles,* Elgar can take the matter no further. He cannot indicate what they must do, and even when he sets the text 'this commandment is for you' the actual commandment is never made explicit. Elgar became more and more depressed at this point after the first three sections had gone to the publishers and he determined to give up the commission altogether. But with help and support from his wife, together with a drastic revision in the scale of the work, he continued composition.

II   AT THE BEAUTIFUL GATE

THE MORN OF PENTECOST

Mary and Mary Magdalene The singers are before the altar; they make sweet melody and sing the words of David, the sweet psalmist; he beautified the feasts that the temple might sound from morning. The Lord hath prepared a sacrifice; the day of the First-Fruits. This man, lame from his mother's womb, is carried daily to the Beautiful Gate; to him that is afflicted pity should he shewed; let us give alms of such things as we have. The blind and the lame came to Jesus in the temple, and He healed them. He knew their sorrows; Himself took their infirmities. and bare their sicknesses. He hath looked down from the height of his sanctuary, to hear their sighing. The service of the Lord is prepared; the day of the First-Fruits: let them go into the house of the Lord

The nature of the scene at the Beautiful Gate on the morning of Pentecost is an intermezzo to follow the complexities of the 'choosing by lots' sequence and the great Pentecost scene that is to come. Elgar places the two Marys at the site where Peter is later to cure the lame man, first mentioned in this section of the oratorio. Once again Elgar put together text from varied sources – the Psalms, Ecclesiasticus, Job, Exodus, as well as Acts – to describe this imagined scene: 'the singers are before the altar' comes from Ecclesiasticus 47:9; 'to him that is afflicted' from Job 6:14. Narrative is kept to a minimum and the text mainly consists of comment but without jarring extremes. Despite his obvious and continuing difficulties with the text, Elgar had learned much since his experience with *The Apostles.* There is also practically nothing obtrusive from the previous work in this limpid but fresh-sounding episode. Familiar themes are delicately woven into the orchestral texture, including the 'Watchers on the Temple Roof' from *The Apostles* and the quotation from *The Light of Life* that points up the miracle of the lame man from Acts 2.

Scene II, 'The Kingdom' From the original manuscript

Elgar consulted Canon Gorton while he was contemplating the scene. The advice offered confirmed Elgar's inventiveness: 'you could if you preferred make it the morn of Pentecost. Again, as to the Beautiful Gate, you are quite right, it was the Gateway which led into the court of the women so that holy women are in place there.'[168] Another suggestion discussed was the equating of Pentecost with 'the day of the First-Fruits'. Where this reference occurs in the text, Elgar uses the *leitmotif* that he gives to 'Pentecost' in the section that follows.

III PENTECOST

IN THE UPPER ROOM

Recit. (Tenor) And when the day of Pentecost was fully come, they were all with one accord in one place.

The Disciple When the great Lord will, we shall be filled with the Spirit of understanding.

Mystic Chorus (Sopranos and Contraltos) The Spirit of the Lord shall rest upon them; the spirit of wisdom and understanding, the spirit of counsel and might, the spirit of knowledge. Come from the four winds, O Spirit!

"I will pour forth of My Spirit, and they shall prophesy; and I will shew wonders in the heaven above, and signs on the earth beneath."

John When the Comforter is come, we shall bear witness;

Peter and speak as moved by the Holy Spirit.

The Disciples When the great Lord will, we shall be filled with the Spirit of understanding.

Recit. (Contralto) And suddenly there came from heaven a sound as of the rushing of a mighty wind, and it filled all the house where they were sitting; and there appeared unto them tongues parting asunder, like as of fire; and it sat upon each one of them: — and they were all filled with the Holy Spirit, and began to speak with other tongues, as the Spirit gave them utterance.

The Disciples He, Who walketh upon the wings of the wind, shall baptise with the Holy Ghost, and with fire, He, whose ministers are flaming fire, shall baptise with the Holy Ghost, and with fire.

Mystic Chorus (Sopranos and Contraltos) (The Lord put forth His hand, and touched their mouth; God hath spoken, who can but prophesy?)

Recit. (Contralto) And there were dwelling in Jerusalem Jews, devout men, from every nation under heaven; and when this sound was heard, the multitude came together, and were all amazed, and marvelled.

The Pentecost scene, in addition to being the central point of the work, by now modified with the approval of the Birmingham Festival authorities to enable completion on time, is also the longest. It is the spiritual crux of the trilogy as Elgar now saw it, where the descent of the Holy Spirit gives Peter his authority, the followers repent, are baptised, and the Church is spread not only throughout Jewry but among the Gentiles. This takes forward the mighty close of *The Apostles* as Christ ascends to Heaven with the promise of his abiding presence. More personally, for the composer, it highlights the reference by the young Elgar's headmaster, Francis Reeve, as he talked about the Apostles: 'perhaps before the descent of the Holy Ghost not [being] cleverer than some of you here'.[169] Elgar chose not to set the narrative directly from Acts 2 which shows the Pentecostal fire coming straight into the assembly in the Upper Room. By intertwining these words (sung as recitatives by the tenor and contralto) with varied texts from the Old Testament he achieves a sense of wonder and awe for the Disciples (the men of the chorus) and a mystic chorus (the women of the chorus). This whole section represents perhaps the most elaborate and imaginative ensemble writing of the whole oratorio. The new text, from Isaiah, Ezekiel and Ecclesiasticus, creates a rare sense of stillness and concentration in which the listener can share the rapt contemplation and ecstasy experienced by the participants in the drama. The movement of the music is continuous but planned in seamless alternating sections, accompanied and unaccompanied.

Then the flame descends from a tranquil resting point in the choral ensemble over a trembling in the orchestra as the contralto sings the words 'and suddenly there came from heaven a sound as of the rushing of a mighty wind'. The orchestration is vivid, the theme itself rushing from top to bottom of the orchestra, the whole reminiscent of the fire music in Wagner's *Die Walküre,* although with very different colouring. The excitement is maintained throughout, including the passing of blazing themes between the men of the chorus over the contralto soloist's continuation of the narrative. This overlapping between narrative and enactment is quite novel. One is in the past tense, the other very much in the present, which produces a two-fold effect. This also creates more immediacy in the scene but, viewed from another perspective, the element of time completely vanishes. There are few references to material from *The Apostles* but the most interesting is a brief acknowledgement of the 'Morning Psalm' in the earlier work, to illustrate the devoutness of the Jews.

IN SOLOMAN'S PORCH

The People Behold are not all these which speak, Galilaeans? And how hear we, every man in our tongue, wherein we were born?

John He, Who walketh upon the wings of the wind, hath baptised with the Holy Ghost, and with fire.

The People We do hear them speak in our tongues the wonderful works of God!

Peter He, Whose ministers are flaming fire, hath baptised with the Holy Ghost, and with fire.

The People What meaneth this? These men are full of new wine. They are truly full of power, even the Spirit of the Lord. They drink, and forget the law, and pervert the judgment. With stammering lips and another tongue will He speak to this people. When they heard, they trembled; like men whom wine hath overcome, their lips quiver. Because of the Lord, and because of the words of His holiness. We hear them speak in our tongues; what meaneth this?

Peter ('I have prayed for thee, that thy faith fail not; and thou, when thou art converted, strengthen thy bretheren.') Ye men of Judaea, and all ye that dwell in Jerusalem, be this known unto you, and give ear to my words: This is that which was spoken by the Prophet, "It shall come to pass in the last days, saith God, I will pour forth of My Spirit upon all flesh: and your sons and your daughters shall prophesy, and your young men shall see visions, and your old men shall dream dreams; and it shall be that whoesover shall call on the Name of the Lord shall be saved." Ye men of Israel, hear these words: Jesus of Nazareth, a Man approved of God unto you by mighty works, and wonders, and signs, which God did by Him in the midst of you, as ye yourselves also know; Him, being delivered up by the determinate counsel and foreknowledge of God, ye, by the hand of lawless men did crucify and slay: this Jesus hath God raised up, whereof we are all witnesses.

Chorus (Sopranos and Contraltos) (The Lord put forth His hand. and touched their mouth; God hath spoken, who can but prophesy?)

Peter Therefore, being exalted at the right hand of God, and having received of the Father the promise of the Holy Ghost, He hath poured forth this, which ye now see and hear. Let all the house of Israel know assuredly, that God hath made Him both Lord and Christ; — this Jesus Whom ye crucified.

The People (Tenors and Basses) ('His blood be on us and on our children.')

Peter Whom ye crucified.

Contralto (Solo) ("Daughters of Jerusalem, weep not for Me. but weep for yourselves, and for your children.")

The People Men and bretheren, what shall we do? We have denied the Holy and Righteous One, and asked for a murderer to be granted to us; we have killed the Prince of life. Men and bretheren, what shall we do?

Peter Repent and be baptised every one of you, in the Name of Jesus Christ; for to you is the promise, and to your children, and to all that are afar off, even as many as the Lord our God shall call unto Him.

The People In the Name of Jesus Christ; for to us is the promise, and to our children and to all that are afar off, even as many as the Lord our God shall call unto Him. Pour upon us the Spirit of grace.

Peter In the Name of Jesus Christ.

The People Pour upon us the Spirit of grace.

All There shall be a fountain opened to the house of David. In the name of Jesus Christ: of His own will, God brought us forth by the word of truth, that we should be a kind of First-Fruits of His creatures, in the Name of Jesus Christ. Whom the God of our fathers hath glorified.

The scene changes to 'Solomon's Porch' in the outer Temple, where people are assembled in great numbers to hear about the miracle of Pentecost. The spiritual centre of The Kingdom has now arrived but the agitation and, to some extent, fear created by the descent of the Holy Spirit is exemplified in the music as the multitude refuses to accept what has happened. Elgar was more than prepared to accept comments, and help, from others at the publishers, Novello, in the absence of August Jaeger, convalescing in Switzerland. John Pointer, a reader with the firm and himself a composer of choral works, proved particularly valuable. He added a restatement of the main 'Apostles' theme in the accompaniment (with Elgar's full approval) over John's confident recitative about Christ baptising those who believe: 'He who walketh upon the wings of the wind'. When Jaeger noticed that the addition had not been orchestrated, Elgar gave no indication about Pointer's help, simply saying: 'I will add this to the score.'[170] Yet John Pointer was instrumental in solving many of Elgar's problems over the piano accompaniment to the oratorio, often producing several versions of various passages from which the composer could choose.

Words which were originally set for Simon of Gitta, about the Apostles being drunk with new wine, are given to the multitude that have yet to be persuaded of the reality of what they have witnessed. Peter has, meanwhile, separated himself from the ensemble to consider, in the light of these momentous events, Christ's promise to strengthen the Apostles' faith so that it may be passed on to others. He now prepares himself to preach. Three heavy brass chords introduce a character filled with a new and greater authority. Music and text are combined with genius in this magnificent oration that, perhaps more than any other section in either *The Apostles* or *The Kingdom,* is immediate and credible. Its appeal is to the emotions, not of an individual but a crowd. This is dangerous ground for an orator. A composer who does not fully understand the setting of declamatory speech to music is bound to fail. Elgar succeeds here because his musical instincts flow with the words almost perfectly.

There has been some criticism that Peter's sermon is weakened by the overuse of past *leitmotifs.* An examination of the original text in Acts 2 reveals that about half the words are from the Old Testament. Elgar felt that quotations from David and Joel would be familiar and appropriate to a Jewish crowd. Part of Joel's prophesy — 'and your young men shall see visions, and your old men shall dream dreams' — was originally set by Elgar to music from the 'Angel's Farewell' from *The Dream of Gerontius* but he revised this just before the full score was printed. The composer felt he had become too preoccupied with the past and that it would be wrong to associate the dreams of an old man with such a forward-looking sermon. The echoes, however, remain.

The people, touched and convinced by Peter's words, confess their guilt at the death of Christ in music of quivering emotional intensity. They repent and are baptised using musical ideas at once haunting, but with great nobility and beauty, which represent the starting point to a large-scale ensemble of ordered dignity. The contrast between this and the choral writing that preceded Peter's address is dramatic.

IV   THE SIGN OF HEALING

AT THE BEAUTIFUL GATE

Recit. (Contralto) Then they that had gladly received his words were baptised, and continued steadfastly in the Apostles teaching, and in Fellowship, in the Breaking of Bread, and the Prayers; and fear came upon every soul, and many wonders and signs were done by the Apostles. The man that was lame, at the Beautiful Gate, seeing Peter and John about to go into the temple, asked to receive alms; and Peter, fastening his eyes upon him, with John, said: –

Peter Look on us. Silver and gold have I none; but what I have, that give I thee. In the Name of Jesus Christ of Nazareth, rise up and walk.

The People This is he which sat for alms, lame from his mother's womb. He entereth the temple, walking and praising God!

Peter Ye men of Israel, why marvel ye at this man? The God of Abraham, of Isaac, and of Jacob, the God of our fathers hath glorified His Servant Jesus, Whom ye delivered up: by faith in His Name hath His Name made this man strong, whom ye behold and know.

John Unto you that fear His Name shall the Sun of righteousness arise with healing in His wings. Unto you first God, having raised up his Servant, sent Him to bless you, in turning away every one of you from your iniquities.

Peter and John Turn ye again, that your sins may be blotted out, that so there may come seasons of refreshing from the presence of the Lord.

A moment of tranquillity follows as a short orchestral introduction returns the next section to the Beautiful Gate of the Temple. The contralto soloist narrates how the conversion and baptism of the people has enabled them to become steadfast in faith. Peter and John perform their first miracle by healing the lame man, which further astonishes the crowd. The strengthened Peter then addresses the people and links the Jewish faith to that of Christ. All this is accompanied by a succession of familiar themes including, once again, the 'Watchers on the Temple Roof' (from *The Apostles*) that throughout *The Kingdom* is closely associated with the Jewish religion. Elgar had much anguish over this relatively short section. It was the first to be written following his return from an extended American tour during which his violent headaches had increased. Further illness and minor accidents prevented him from working properly at a time when the oratorio should have been nearly completed. He was attempting to show, for the first and only time in *The Kingdom,* Peter's power in a practical sense. What emerged was over almost before it had begun, with little drama. Looking back a mere ten years it would surely have been obvious that almost the whole of a previous oratorio – *The Light of Life* – had been created out of just such a happening. Perhaps Elgar *was* looking back. The duets between Peter and John in this section, while lyrical and impassioned, do not fit easily with the overall style of *The Kingdom.* They are much more akin to the earlier work and come from discarded sketches for *The Light of Life.*

THE ARREST

Recit. (Contralto) And as they spake, the priests and the Sadducees came upon them, being sore troubled, because they proclaimed in Jesus the resurrection from the dead: and they laid hands on them, and put them in ward unto the morrow; for it was now eventide.

Mary The sun goeth down; Thou makest darkness. and it is night: I commune with mine own heart. and meditate on Thee in the night watches. Blessed are ye when men shall persecute you for His sake. They deliver them up to the council, they are hated of men for His Name's sake; all this is come upon them: – some shall they kill and crucify; blessed are ye, reproached for the Name of Christ. Rejoice, ye partakers of His sufferings, that when His glory shall be revealed ye may be glad also, with exceeding joy. How great are Thy signs, how mighty are Thy wonders; Who healeth all infirmities. The Gospel of the Kingdom shall be preached in the whole world; the Kingdom and the patience which are in Jesus. The Branch of the Lord shall be beautiful and glorious. Thou makest darkness, I meditate on Thee; in the night Thy song shall be with me a prayer unto the God of my life.

Peter and John's arrest by the priests and Sadducees for openly preaching the resurrection of the dead through Jesus is recounted by the contralto soloist. Two things appealed to Elgar in this scene. The first was the memory that some ten years earlier, in *The Light of Life,* he had once again depicted punishment for the working of a miracle; the second was surely the final words of the Biblical quotation from Acts 4 sung by the contralto: 'for it was now eventide'. This provided the cue for the longest solo in either *The Apostles* or *The Kingdom* where Jesus's grieving mother sings of anguished suffering and tremendous hope against the onset of another night. The text was taken almost line-by-line from many Old and New Testament sources to point up, once again, an expression of Elgar's own despair.

Working on this passage epitomised the overall problem with the two oratorios. As a symphonist at heart, the most ideal way of portraying the sunset would be through the orchestra. Yet the drama and emotion that the scene needed to evoke could only really be achieved in words. It was the juxtaposition of these elements – drama and music – that caused him so much concern. Everything here, however, is perfectly balanced. This is a nocturne full of withdrawn and troubled sweetness, yet soaring to heights that Elgar perhaps never reached again through such a medium. It matches Peter's earlier sermon and remains, to many, the very heart of Elgar.

The first 'verse' of the solo uses words mainly from the Psalms (the title itself, 'The Sun Goeth Down', comes from Psalm 104:20) but the central focus sets text taken from the 'Persecution' and 'Persecution of the Righteous' sections in *The Topical Bible*. Unusually, at a time of such despair, Elgar at last felt able to set the missing ninth Beatitude – about being reviled – into this soliloquy using the same theme given to the Virgin Mary in the Beatitudes section of *The Apostles*. There are nine Beatitudes in Chapter 5 of St Matthew's Gospel and Elgar set them all in *The Apostles* with the exception of 'Blessed art thou when men shall revile you and persecute you and say all manner of evil against you falsely for my sake'. He could not bring himself to do this, as rejection of his music, and the personal humiliation that would result, weighed heavily on his mind to the end of his life. Even when, as a dying man in 1934, he spoke despairingly to Ernest Newman of his fear that his music would not survive him, it became clear just how deep that feeling ran. A new Beatitude, which continues the suffering and persecution idea, is also inserted in the text of the soliloquy. This comes from the first of Peter's Epistles. The final exultant verses are taken from St Matthew and Revelation and include, for only the second time in the work, the word 'Kingdom'. Elgar had very strong feelings about the proper translation of 'the Kingdom and the patience' in the simultaneous German text as he was convinced that the important sense had somehow been lost. The composer wrote to Novello just before the premiere; 'will you please *insist* that *Patience* must be in even if we alter the phrasing of the music completely.'[171] This insistence stemmed from his own researches in the *Luther Bible*, where the word 'Geduld' is appropriately used.

It is difficult, and not very satisfactory, to analyse the music of the soliloquy. Some say it almost defies analysis but Elgar's highly imaginative use of the violin solo to introduce extracts from the Jewish *Hymn of Weeping* ('Al Elleh') and later, the *Hymn of Parting* ('Ham abdil') that underline Mary's opening private meditation must be mentioned. Elgar consulted Rabbi Cohen, who described the first of them as an 'example of the plaintive elegies chanted, or rather crooned, in the dim-lighted synagogue on the fatal 9th of Ab, the anniversary of the destruction of both Temples'.[172] The haunting violin solo which opens the soliloquy quietly closes it. What listeners have experienced within the space of some 130 bars is, perhaps, the strongest highlight of the whole oratorio. The impression of a lonely figure set against the descending night sky is what remains indelibly.

V THE UPPER ROOM

IN FELLOWSHIP

The Disciples and the Holy Women The voice of joy is in the dwelling of the righteous: the stone which the builders rejected is become the head of the corner.

John The rulers asked: "By what power, or in what name, have ye done this?" Then Peter, filled with the Holy Spirit, said "In the Name of Jesus Christ."

The Disciples and the Holy Women In none other is there salvation: neither is there, under heaven, any other name wherein we must be saved.

Peter And when they took knowledge of us that we had been with Jesus, they charged us not to speak at all, nor teach in His Name; we cannot but speak the things we saw and heard.

John Finding nothing how they might punish us, concerning a good deed done to an impotent man, they further threatened us; and being let go, we are come to our own company.

The Disciples and the Holy Women Lord, Thou didst make the heaven, and the earth, and the sea, and all that in them is. The rulers gather together against the Lord and his Anointed: Lord behold their threatenings; grant Thy servants to speak Thy word with all boldness, while Thou stretchest forth Thy hand to heal. Praise the Name of our God That hath dealt wondrously with us.

The two Apostles are released from prison and the final scene takes place once again in the Upper Room. They both detail their cross-examination before the chief Priests and elders. Elgar experienced some difficulties with this passage, as he explained to Canon Gorton, in August 1906: 'I have a terrible moment when Peter says "they took knowledge of us that *we had been with Jesus*" . . . here there is a momentary suggestion of the Denial & the Servants: an instantaneous revelation of Peter's mind impossible in any other art than music.'[173] Listeners may, however, be puzzled by the fervour of the rejoicing which came from the overnight imprisonment of the two Apostles.

But clearly the interest has now been lost and the ending of the work makes little overall impression in the way that much of the previous material has. The abrupt interruption of the chorus into Peter and John's account of their interrogation is curious and the purpose of the words starting: 'Lord, Thou didst make the heaven, and the earth, and the sea' is not altogether clear at this point. Elgar, perhaps wisely, chose to depict the 'threatenings' of the Chief Priests and Elders by selecting less obvious text than that from Acts 4: 'Why did the heathen rage, and the people imagine a vain thing.'

THE BREAKING OF BREAD

The Disciples and the Holy Women Thou, Almighty Lord, hast given food and drink to mankind; but to us, Thou hast vouchsafed spiritual food and drink and life eternal through Thy Servant.

Peter If any is holy: —

The Disciples let him come.

Peter If any is not: —

The Disciples and the Holy Women let him repent.

Mary, Mary Magdalene, John and Peter In the Name of Jesus Christ.

John Give thanks, — first for the Cup.

The Disciples and the Holy Women We thank Thee, our Father, for the Holy Vine.

Peter Give thanks: — for the Broken Bread.

The Disciples and the Holy Women We thank Thee, our Father, for the Life and Knowledge. As this Broken Bread was grain scattered upon the mountains, and gathered together became one, so may Thy Church be gathered together from the bounds of the earth into Thy Kingdom.

It is not until the whole spirit of the music changes and settles – 'The Breaking of Bread' – that Elgar appears to be back in control. This, however, cannot fully compensate for such a noticeable lapse of interest. Once again the vehicle for the change is the Gregorian antiphon *O sacrum convivium*. Choosing not to set the Church's Eucharistic and Biblically based prayers, because this would have put a priest's words into a layman's mouth, Elgar used instead the *Didache,* a second-century prayer manual discovered at a Constantinople Monastery in 1873.

> ## THE PRAYERS
>
> *All* Our Father, Which art in Heaven, hallowed be Thy Name; Thy Kingdom come, Thy will be done on earth as it is in Heaven. Give us this day our daily bread; and forgive us our trespasses, as we forgive them that trespass against us, and lead us not into temptation, but deliver us from evil: for Thine is the Kingdom, the power, and the glory; for ever and ever, Amen.
>
> *John* Ye have received the Spirit of adoption,
>
> *Peter* whereby we cry, Abba, —
>
> *Men* Father
>
> *All* Thou, O Lord, art our Father, our Redeemer, and we are Thine.

From this point Elgar uses his setting of the Lord's Prayer written three years earlier but unused in *The Apostles.* It is highly emotional, chromatic writing and not altogether in place here. The music rises above the emotion only at the words 'for Thine is the glory for ever and ever' but this expected climax, which could have concluded the oratorio in a conventional manner, is not maintained. Instead the work ends with a quiet 'Amen' over the restatement of familiar themes. This is a figurative sigh of relief on Elgar's part at having succeeded in completing the drastically revised scheme. He could clearly no longer carry on with the pain which his failure to achieve the magnificent original vision of the Apostles trilogy had created. There was, of course, to be no more large-scale religious choral writing from his pen and perhaps he knew that even then. Alice Elgar summed it all up succinctly in her diary: 'E: really finished the composing of his beautiful work — Most thankful.'[174]

CHAPTER FOURTEEN

THE PUBLISHED SCORES OF
'THE KINGDOM'

The manuscript vocal score, Elgar's first stage in ordered composition of the work, bears neither title nor opus number. What became the Prelude was called 'Introduction' (even on Elgar's manuscript full orchestral score) and the piano setting of this opening section was completed on 11 January 1906. Satisfactory progress was maintained into the chorus 'O Ye Priests!' which followed the choosing of a new Apostle to replace Judas and Elgar also sent his setting of the Lord's Prayer, completed three years earlier, to the publishers as the ending to the oratorio's first part. By the end of January, however, he was in crisis with Alice Elgar noting in her diary that 'E thinking cd. not finish his work'.[175] Following negotiations with Novello and Birmingham Festival authorities about reducing the oratorio's scope, Elgar resumed work in the latter part of February but without much real enthusiasm. On 27 March he had reached the end of the 'Pentecost Scene' and sent this to Novello & Co. before leaving for America. Elgar also played the completed parts of the oratorio to R H Wilson, chorus-master of the Birmingham Triennial Festival, who is said to have been 'impressed beyond measure'.[176]

Novello & Co. had been sending vocal score proofs to Elgar in Hereford since 16 January and he requested that 'everything possible'[177] be sent to him either in Cincinnati or New York. Despite distractions at the Cincinnati Country Club, where the Elgars were staying, and the strain of his conducting engagements, Elgar began orchestrating the oratorio on 19 April. His enthusiasm for this task meant that before returning to England at the end of May, Novello had received some 65 pages of full orchestral score. There is some evidence to suggest that he had actually completed almost 100 pages before his return. Unlike in *The Apostles,* Elgar would not agree to the string parts being engraved by Geidel in Leipzig without the benefit of a performance and therefore William Dodd of Kew undertook the work. In this respect, at least, progress on the new oratorio showed a significant advance over that of the former work.

But Elgar's depression returned when he started further work on the score. He spent most of his birthday, 2 June, in bed. It was not until 20 June, during an enforced holiday at New Radnor ordered by his doctor, that serious composition began again and five days later he assured Novello & Co. that the work would be completed by the end of July. Printing could continue throughout August and the chorus would be able to learn the remaining portions in September. With difficulty the agreed timetable was kept to and the manuscript vocal score completed on 23 July despite Elgar having had a fall and suffering with a painful knee. Orchestration was resumed on 29 July and proceeded with remarkable speed. Novello & Co. received a parcel on 8 August bringing the number of pages to 168. The total had reached 200 only two days later and Alice Elgar wrote anxiously to Jaeger (recently returned from convalescence in Switzerland) about the lack of vocal score proofs from which to judge the layout of the full orchestral score and rule the staves ready for

The title page of 'The Kingdom'.

orchestration. It is clear that Elgar was proceeding so fast that her preparations were faltering. The end of the oratorio (page 362) was reached on 31 August and the final batch of material sent to Novello that day.

Proof copies of the full score had been arriving since July and with corrections agreed William Dodd could now update some of the orchestral parts. Time was short, though, and Agnes Nicholls, Elgar's chosen soprano who was to sing the part of the Virgin Mary, wrote to Jaeger on 16 August asking for 'a rough proof of my "big" scene – then it will have time to simmer'.[178] Dodd sent the completed string parts to Novello on 7 September but knew that he could get little further than the end of the 'Pentecost Scene' with other parts as the volume was too great for one man; it would eventually require two extra copyists to finish the work in time. Elgar was concurrently checking the string parts, working on them with the assistance of John Austin from Worcester. On 11 September he was so preoccupied that he would not go with the rest of the household to a Three Choirs Festival performance of *The Dream of Gerontius*. Alice Elgar noted five days later that 'Mr Austin arrived before 3. & all worked hard – Mr Kilburn played, E. played the violin, Mrs Worthington turned over'.[179] Nicholas Kilburn recalled the occasion as follows: 'With the piano score it was interesting to watch how Sir Edward "spotted" the printer's mistakes, and how dexterously he and Mr Austin played the various parts including, of course, those of the transposing instruments'.[180] By the end of that day Elgar appeared satisfied with the string parts as far as the end of 'At the Beautiful Gate'. On 22 and 23 September Elgar was still engrossed in the work with Austin and the following day the completed string parts were handed to Novello by Geidel's London agent. This was only one day before the first orchestral rehearsal at Belle Vue, Manchester. Alice Elgar wrote to Jaeger on 26 September about the 'gorgeous sea of sound . . . the band broke now & again into irresistible applause'.[181]

Elgar's Prelude to *The Kingdom* points the way to the superb scoring of the whole oratorio. The manuscript vocal score contains only three indications about the subsequent scoring – the audacious writing for four horns with viola and cello during the scene 'In Solomon's Porch' which had been in his mind since 17 February when he wrote to Adolf Borsdorf, first horn in the London Symphony Orchestra, about its practicality; where the trumpets emerge strikingly from the texture later in the same scene; the use of the violin solos in the Virgin Mary's soliloquy.

Despite his depressions, Elgar's certainty over the eventual composition meant very few errors in the manuscript vocal score. Jaeger criticised two bars in the Prelude and these were changed. John Pointer at Novello suggested an additional counterpoint for one of the scenes to which Elgar agreed. But the most significant alteration was to the passage in Peter's sermon, 'and your young men shall see visions, and your old men dream dreams'. It is, perhaps, easy to see why the second phrase should evoke memories of *The Dream of Gerontius* and that he should, therefore set it nostalgically to music from the 'Angel's Farewell'. But what of the young men? Perhaps he was still one of them, visionary though he might be, but could Peter at this point really afford to look back? The quotation was abandoned, but long after the original setting had been fully scored. Even then it was not to be pasted over – the new version was added as an insert.

Unlike that of *The Apostles,* the full score of *The Kingdom* was from the outset to be published with a German translation. In February 1906 Novello approached Julian Buths, loyal Elgarian and conductor of the Lower Rhine Festival, who had already translated *The Dream of Gerontius* and *The Apostles.* He was sent Alice Elgar's typescript of the first scene, containing several wrong Biblical references which led to a great deal of confusion. At the beginning of August, when part of the translation had been engraved into the score, Buths heard via Jaeger that Elgar had criticised several later passages of translation and suggested an urgent meeting in Hereford, but Elgar was too busy. Ten days after the premiere Elgar was still worried about the translation problems because Buths had used the Lutheran Bible with a freedom which exceeded Elgar's own in the case of the Authorized Version. The composer insisted that certain words were essential. *Gelduld* (patience) has already been mentioned in the previous chapter but he also questioned *Bauleuten* (builders) — *'builders* should certainly go in or the "idea" fails'.[182] Elgar's opinion prevailed but he was unsuccessful with Buths over the German title for the work. Deeply unhappy with the political overtones of 'Das Reich' he urged 'Das Reich Gottes' but brevity and consistency won the day.

Research for the latest edition of the full orchestral score revealed 303 errors that needed correction. When, however, the first printed full score eventually reached Elgar on 15 June 1907, he acknowledged it to Novello with 'thanks and admiration . . . it is really a splendid "book", the printing could not be better & is worthy of the glorious Hall in Wardour Street from which it comes'.[183]

CHAPTER FIFTEEN

'THE LAST JUDGEMENT'
(THE UNWRITTEN ORATORIO)

Elgar's colleagues and friends were aware of many possible titles for the third, unwritten, oratorio of the trilogy – *The Saints, The Fulfilment, The Judgement, The Vision, The Throne, The Holy City* – but it seems likely that the one written on the cover of the file of sketches at Elgar's death was definitive – *The Last Judgement,* although for many years he favoured *The Saints* as a title.

A pencilled note may give an idea of Elgar's approach to the work as a whole when he quotes the words from Jeremiah 10: 'For the pastors are become brutish & have not sought the Lord.'[184] This was the exact opposite of the original driving force behind the Apostles themselves. Research by the composer had been widening over the years since *The Kingdom* and, despite Elgar's public and private statements about not completing the trilogy, a copy of R. H. Charles's *Lectures on the Apocalypse* was obtained. Alice Elgar clearly disapproved of James New's *Traditional Aspects of Hell* having a prominent place in Elgar's study. He also used ideas from Bousset's *The Antichrist Legend,* noting certain links between Judaism and such obscure subjects as 'the Babylonian Dragon myth'; 'Ninip in the Armarna tablets'; 'Ninurta, the war god of Mesopotamia'. All these, and many more, are marked up as possible cross-references. From Farrar's *The Early Days of Christianity* he queried a possible connection between the 'Wild Beast of Revelation' and the emperor Nero. He also highlighted many references from Revelation in Renan's *Antichrist* (1899) and wrote on the flyleaf 'Shofar = Last Trumpet eternal dawn'[185] to link this potential closing scene with the opening of *The Apostles.* Also noted on the flyleaf is a Seneca quotation found in St Augustine's *The City of God:* 'Victi victoribus leges dederunt' (the conquered gave laws to the conquerors).[186]

He had relied heavily on Pinnock's *Analysis of New Testament History* throughout all the work undertaken on the Apostles project. It is, therefore, not surprising that Elgar's copy of this book has copious notes appended about Revelation. Of particular interest is the point where 'Shofar'[187] is written twice when the author discusses the seventh trumpet. Pinnock also had a view that the 'Man of Sin' referred to in Revelation was actually the Pope and that the 'Apostasy' was to be found in the 'abominable corruptions of the Roman Catholic Church'. Elgar's undisguised 'Hurrah!'[188] in the page's margin is telling indeed.

Some detailed text was compiled. John was seen as representing 'The Spirit of Trusting Love' and Peter 'The Spirit of Robust Faith'. There appear to be no properly defined characterisations apart from these brief comments, although a pencilled 'peter'[189] [sic] is written against the section from Charles's *Lectures on the Revelation* when the author quotes 'For the Lamb that is in the midst of the throne shall be their shepherd . . . And God shall wipe away all tears from their eyes'. Drafts and sketches exist and from these it is possible to say that certain elements were to be included. Among the written notes on the final oratorio is a letter in draft to a Rev. W. E. Ton in which Elgar describes the work as 'beginning with the Strife – Anti-Christ (a logical progression from Judas through the unset Simon Magus episodes to the final challenge against Christ's authority) – and concluding with the Apocalypse (judgment) and the Kingdom of Heaven'.[190] The idea of 'judgement' is highlighted in a letter from Capel-Cure in which he urges Elgar not to 'forget there is a magnificent "Song of the Sword" . . . which may do for your concluding oratorio. I should like to see it "Furbished that it may glitter" in your moving music.'[191] The quotation comes from Ezekiel 11: 'A sword, a sword is sharpened, and also furbished: It is sharpened to make a sore slaughter: it is furbished that it may glitter.'

Many years earlier Elgar had a friend, Minnie Baker, arrange a text from St Augustine's *Civitas Dei* for a choral work. This was never used but formed the basis of Elgar's thinking about the final 'Heavenly Kingdom' scenes. It is from the sketches for this section particularly that much of the *Last Judgement* material eventually worked into the projected Third Symphony can be traced. Among these is a fragment which sets text from Revelation 9:1 – 'Alleluia. Salvation and glory, and power belong to our God' – in a slightly amended form. Of the others, perhaps the most significant are a pounding second 'Antichrist' theme used to open the symphony; a sketch titled 'Hell followed him'[192] from the scene of the fourth seal which occurs in the first movement's development; a viola solo in the symphony's second movement which derives from a projected tenor solo (words not specified), probably St John; a passage which finds its way into several Elgar sketchbooks and on which he was working at his death called 'The Judgement'[193] to start the symphony's slow movement – there is some indication that this theme would have been used to open the oratorio and an idea (adagio) called 'Apoc[alypse]'[194] in which the word 'Shofar'[195] is pencilled which would associate it with the Last Trumpet and the seventh angel to herald the 'eternal dawn' at the conclusion of the work. The composer Anthony Payne took the 130 pages of completed sketches for the Third Symphony and, between 1995 and 1997, constructed a 'realisation' of the work that was premiered by the BBC Symphony Orchestra. It is now possible, together with music for *The Spanish Lady*, to hear at least some small fragments of Elgar's intentions for his final oratorio on the Apostles theme.

But the major problem, as ever, was actually compiling the text. Much is based upon the last chapters of Acts and the book of Revelation. Dialogue is noticeably absent in both of these sources and, given the problems Elgar had experienced with his librettos for *The Apostles* and *The Kingdom,* it seems likely that discouragement over this point alone would have deflected him from attempting the conclusion.

The choral prologue came from Daniel 7. A second scene includes the material for Cornelius, the Centurion who became the first Gentile convert in Acts 10. The book of Revelation appears extensively in both the text and musical sketches. There are queries in the notebooks about 'Cornelius', 'blind man', 'Peter imprisoned', 'Antioch'.[196]

Elgar's work on Simon Magus, largely prompted by Longfellow, resulted in an almost complete libretto for his scenes but the music eventually found its way into Elgar's unfinished opera *The Spanish Lady* (completed in a realisation by Dr Percy Young and published by Novello, 1995). Some 70 bars are used in a duet between the characters Meercraft and Everill. Meercraft, as Elgar describes him, is 'a plausible rogue who will take anyone's money',[197] and Everill is 'his cousin debauched'.[198] Both, like their source, Simon Magus, are obsessed with money and its potential power.

Consideration of the Antichrist idea appears in odd notes and sometimes in unusual places. Even on the back of a programme for the 1914 Three Choirs Festival at Worcester, Elgar records a quotation from Isaiah 5, where he notes: 'contained: some vivid stuff, maybe for Antichrist Sc.'[199] and an underlined verse which includes the words: 'he will lift up an ensign to the nations from far, and will hiss unto them from the end of the earth'.[200]

Yet another sequence that was sketched out included the opening of the seals from Revelation 6. This scene is predominantly a fiery exchange between John and the chorus. The male chorus's repeated interjection 'Come!' is enlarged by 'as a voice with thunder' at which point Elgar added in pencil to the libretto typescript '(G.C. [Large Gong] with near shattering steel).'[201] The musical sketch shows also the apocalyptic use of the bass drum and double basses divided into four parts. When the fourth seal is opened, John describes Death as 'the rider of a pale horse'. The chorus text at this point, 'And hell followed with him', comes from two separate sources. As Elgar explained, in a note with the sketches, he had used the word 'Hell' from the Authorized Version of the Bible but the other text comes from the Revised version: 'I know this is wrong, the dead limbs are meant but Hell is too good to lose.'[202] An interesting comment about the style of the music is also appended here: 'Demons Geront'.[203] Would he have taken a quotation from the 'Demon's Chorus' in *The Dream of Gerontius*? At the opening of the fifth seal the words given to John are: 'I saw underneath the altar the souls of them that had been slain for the word of God'. The last six words are circled by Elgar and a note indicates 'Mary's vision "Kingdom"'.[204] This refers to Mary's soliloquy 'The Sun Goeth Down' in *The Kingdom*.

From the same pencilled notes he links the 'Barren women', stemming from Judas through Sapphira in Acts 12. This scene was originally destined for *The Kingdom* but deleted at the first major revision. References to women abound elsewhere and he queried 'Rise up, ye women that are at ease; hear my voice, ye careless daughters'[205] from Isaiah 32. He even considered the 'Cannibal mothers' from 2 Kings 6. Some references are linked with the 'Barren fig tree' cursed by Christ.

Despite Elgar's assertion to August Jaeger in 1906 that the music for *The Last Judgement* was at least partly written, it now seems clear that this was not actually the case. What did exist remained as either sketches or ideas in the composer's mind.

Only one typewritten sketch of proposed text exists:

> *John* And I saw when the Lamb opened one of the seven seals, and I heard one of the four living creatures say as with a voice of thunder [Rev 6:1]
>
> *Chorus* Come!
>
> *John* And I saw, and behold, a white horse, [Rev 6:2]

Chorus And he that sat thereon had a bow, and then was given unto him a crown; and he came forth conquering and to conquer. [Rev 6:2]

John And when he opened the second seal, I heard the second living creature say, [Rev 6:3]

Chorus Come!

John And another horse came forth, a red horse [Rev 6:4]

Chorus And to him that sat thereon it was given to take peace from the earth, and that they should slay one another: and there was given unto him a great sword [Rev 6:4]

John And when he opened the third seal, I heard the third living creature say, [Rev 6:5]

Chorus Come!

John And I beheld, and lo, a black horse [Rev 6:6]

Chorus And he that sat thereon had a balance in his hand and I heard a voice saying, A measure of wheat for a penny, and three measures of barley for a penny, and the oil and wine hurt thou not [Rev 6:6]

John And when he opened the fourth seal, I heard the voice of the [fourth] living creature say, [Rev 6:7]

Chorus Come!

John And I saw, and behold, a pale horse: and he that sat upon him, his name was DEATH [Rev 6:8]

Chorus And Hell followed with him. And power was given unto them to kill with the sword, and with famine, and with pestilence, and the wild beasts of the earth. [Rev 6:9]

John And when he opened the fifth seal, I saw underneath the altar the souls of them that had been slain for the word of God [Rev 6:9]

Male chorus for 'The Opening of the Seals' (sketch from 'The Last Judgement')

(2)

77

CHORUS.

Rev. 6. COME !

JOHN.

And I beheld, and lo, a black horse:

CHORUS.

And he that sat thereon had a balance in his hand.

6.   And I heard a voice saying % .   A measure of ~~wheat~~

wheat for a penny, and three measures of barley for a

penny; and the oil and wine hurt thou not.

JOHN.

7.   And when he opened the fourth seal, I heard the voice

of the ~~third~~ fourth living creature say,

CHORUS.

COME !

JOHN.

8.   And I saw, and behold, a pale horse; and he that sat

~~thereon~~ upon him, his name was DEATH;

CHORUS.

And Hell followed with ~~with~~ him. And power was given

unto them .   .   to kill with the sword, and with

famine, and with pestilence, and by the wild beasts of

the earth.

JOHN.

9.   And when hn opened the fifth seal, I saw underneath the

altar the souls of them that had been slain for the word

of God

Libretto notes for 'The Opening of the Seals' (from 'The Last Judgement')

116

The passage appears to contain no real narrative frame; and, unlike his role in *The Kingdom*, John is not speaking to any other characters. What the fragment shows clearly is that both John and the chorus share equal knowledge about the opening of the seals and complement each other's phrases so as to give the impression of speaking directly to audience. If criticism about Elgar's text being somewhat conceited *can* be levelled at *The Apostles* and *The Kingdom*, he has come some distance here where the chorus is being used to tell their story directly and without the necessity for narrative.

The use of textual material such as this would represent a radical departure from Elgar's previous oratorio characterisations. In his four, large-scale, 'Biblical' works Elgar portrays, in an entirely convincing way, what might be called 'human reactions' – the grief of a mother and the suffering of a blind man *(The Light of Life)*, the suffering and death of a worldly man *(The Dream of Gerontius)*, the reaction of Mary Magdalene and Judas to their own 'sins' *(The Apostles)*, both the Virgin Mary's and John's reactions to the crucifixion of Christ *(The Kingdom)* and the Virgin Mary's reaction to the arrest of John and Peter *(The Kingdom)*. With *The Last Judgement* it is more than possible that all the characters would be 'immortal' (this would include John and any other Apostle who 'returned') thereby drawing attention away from human reactions. Who now could Elgar use in his well-known concern for the human condition? Would it be the 'suffering masses' in thrall to the Antichrist? Following the Apocalypse, how could Elgar return to any spirit of hope and peace in Heaven? It is clear that a completely different approach would have been required – radically changed from his original concept for the telling of Apostles story.

PART THREE

'I am not sure if I shall ever complete my task
but it is the one work to which
I devote my best thought.'

Edward Elgar

THE
APOSTLES TRILOGY
IN RETROSPECT

CHAPTER SIXTEEN

THE END OF THE
ENGLISH ORATORIO TRADITION?

E lgar's Apostles concept took on a Wagnerian dimension right from the start. Before that he had, in *The Dream of Gerontius,* shown a true understanding of Wagner's ability to give magnificent conclusions to each of the acts in a drama. Why was he so unable to do this in the two completed oratorios of the Apostles trilogy? Was it really the text that confounded him in the end or, more probably, the fact that all his detailed research into the Bible and the many commentaries actually reduced, rather than strengthened, his faith, which was his original intention through these works? Whatever their shortcomings, Elgar's musical genius makes them almost convincing, despite the fact that many more than the three projected oratorios would have been needed to fulfil his vision.

As with Vaughan Williams's *The Pilgrim's Progress* experience, Elgar might have spent too long thinking about the scheme he intended to make his life's work. Gerald Finzi had similar difficulties with the gestation of his *Intimations of Immortality.* Identity with the subject does not always produce the objectivity to present it coherently. The heart of all three composers is, however, to be found within these, their longest and most complex, works. It is right to echo Michael Kennedy's thoughts that *The Apostles* and *The Kingdom,* like *The Pilgrim's Progress* can be seen as: 'music by great composers, although they do not produce music which is consistently great'.[206] If Elgar's genius is sometimes lost in the vastness of *The Apostles* it re-emerges in *The Kingdom* despite his, by now, growing sense of failure over the project as a whole. But what the later oratorio unerringly points to is the symphonic skill in which his future success was to lie.

Perhaps the main problem with *The Apostles* remains that the many *leitmotifs* introduced and constantly reused are very rarely developed fully. Ernest Newman, always at his most critical where Elgar's later choral music was concerned, commented that these fragments often 'succeed one another in obedience, not to musical, but merely to literary or pictorial suggestions'.[207] August Jaeger maintained that these themes were 'woven into the texture'[208] but this is not actually the case. They are, for the most part, 'pasted together', but in a masterly and almost seamless way. The joins do not often show. Elgar's genius in this highly unorthodox method of working is surely without equal.

The two major character portraits, Mary Magdalene and Judas, are framed by the rather more pastoral episodes – 'By the Wayside' and 'At the Sepulchre'. There is a powerful opening in The Calling of the Apostles, and a superbly mystical ending in The Ascension. This produces a strongly unified whole but the best parts of the work throw into even sharper relief those sections where Elgar has lost his imagination or where the inspiration is subsumed into facile consecutive statements of the main musical themes. Elgar's preoccupation with the theological aspects of the oratorio, so as not to give offence, perhaps sometimes made him willing to sacrifice development for the sake of such acceptability. Despite this, however, the work remains a truly great, if neglected, achievement for a composer so at odds with himself during its composition.

In structure *The Kingdom* appears clearer and more simple as the action takes place over a shorter period of time. The scope is less panoramic. There are fewer vocally complex episodes, although the orchestration remains central to describing events and is quite opulent. Overall there is perhaps less richness in contrast than with *The Apostles* but the message of *The Kingdom* can be seen as more direct and less mystic than the earlier work. Elgar confirmed this in a letter to Jaeger: 'The whole thing is intentionally less mystic than the A! – the *men* are alive & working & the atmosphere is meant to be more direct & simple.'[209]

Other problems remain, and these are unavoidable. Many of the *leitmotifs* used in *The Apostles* appear in *The Kingdom,* but with Christ and Judas gone from the scene, listeners can be reminded of earlier actions only through these themes. By developing such fragments Elgar, for the most part, succeeds in transforming them into something more powerful. This is necessary if listeners are to be convinced that the Apostles have now become men of action inspired by their past experiences. However, removal of the central characters does make *The Kingdom* less dramatic and emotionally moving.

Overall, Elgar had come little distance in time with *The Kingdom* and, compared with the momentous events in *The Apostles*, very little had actually happened. There were improvements, though, and Elgar's writing for chorus surpasses that of *The Apostles,* playing a much bigger part in the overall layout and impact of the oratorio. It has been suggested that such fine choral writing may actually overshadow the brilliant orchestrations which listeners often take for granted.

The temptation to consider Elgar's oratorios as 'rehearsals' for his symphonic works has to be avoided. The traditional view that Elgar's earlier compositions are a natural upward progression is understandable. His contemporaries regarded the symphony as the 'pinnacle of musical art' and he must clearly have been under pressure from his friends and critics to produce such a work. Also, as work on *The Apostles* and *The Kingdom* produced so much stress, together with the 'unfinished' state of each work compared with his original scheme and the fact that both oratorios were only completed relatively close to the date of their premieres, it is not surprising that Elgar wished to distance himself from large-scale choral works.

In any event, after 1906 he became busier than ever with a variety of other projects. The Birmingham Festival made no offer of a commission for 1909 and Elgar did not seek one. He continued to amass material of various sorts until 1922 but could not, apparently, sustain interest in *The Last Judgement* for any period of time. Following Alice Elgar's death in 1920, he completed fewer large-scale compositions, preferring to conduct and record his own music. By 1932, the Apostles Trilogy had been abandoned completely. Elgar's work on his opera – *The Spanish Lady* based on Ben Jonson's *The Devil is an Ass*, on a third symphony and sketches for a piano concerto used a great deal of the musical material from the projected *The Last Judgement*. Both of these projects were, however, huge undertakings for an ageing composer and Elgar died in 1934 with them incomplete.

Despite Elgar's feelings of failure over the two completed oratorios of the Apostles Trilogy, it is worth considering whether, if *The Last Judgement* had been written, it would have been the relative success that *The Dream of Gerontius, The Apostles* and *The Kingdom* were. After the First World War major changes in both the production of music festivals and in music technology were taking place. Also, the Birmingham Triennial Festival was never staged after 1912 although other festivals did continue following the war. Their emphasis had, however, in most cases changed because, among many other casualties of the 1914-18 conflict, choirs had been decimated. In any event, even prior to 1910, orchestral music had begun to replace the choral tradition. This tendency increased during the inter-war years as a rapidly maturing musical nation, Britain's musicians, critics, educated audiences and even composers became increasingly suspicious of choral music. Perhaps this was unavoidable because, during the late nineteenth century, choral music was developing in different ways. Traditionally the middle-class had taken the lead with such music for the great festivals. Now, an increasing number of works were produced for temperance choirs, working men's groups, competitive festivals, and even working-class children.

'The sense of paternalism and class patronage, which led the upper and middle classes to embrace the oratorio as a panacea for working-class ills in the nineteenth century, transformed itself into class snobbery when the working classes finally began participating in choral singing and even producing their own new choral music.'[210]

Recording technology also played a part in the decline of oratorio. Gramophone records and radio broadcasts were becoming more popular and these favoured the recording of instrumental works. Before 1925, by using the 'acoustic process', performers gathering around a relatively small 'horn' for recording purposes were easier to cope with than the larger numbers and greater space required for most oratorios. These difficulties had a direct effect on Elgar who remained under contract to HMV. He had suggested a complete recording of *The Dream of Gerontius* in 1918, but this project had not been taken forward as the engineers remained doubtful about their ability adequately to reproduce the choruses and the length of the composition. Clearly, these problems did not apply to his instrumental works: the Second Symphony was recorded complete using the acoustic process in 1924, as were the Cello and Violin Concertos. When the electric recording process was introduced in 1925, choral music was rarely recorded. Recordings of symphonies and operas increased rapidly but the choral repertoire remained largely untouched. Selections from *The Dream of Gerontius* and *The Music Makers,* and the orchestral Prelude from *The Kingdom,* appeared in the HMV catalogue but no complete performances were recorded. The BBC too seemed to favour instrumental music. From 1922, when broadcasting started, they sponsored their own orchestra but had no direct choral forces until 1928.

The oratorio, which had been a hallmark of British musical life, was gone. A third Apostles oratorio from Elgar may have been welcomed out of nostalgia but the composer's post-1906 instrumental tendencies, together with the decline of the music festival and new technologies, would have made its popularity difficult. Where they survived, larger festivals continued to offer choral commissions but, in reality, any major choral work from this time forward was usually written for a specific occasion rather than a music festival.

Consequently, and in spite of his later intentions, Elgar's relative success with *The Apostles* and *The Kingdom* remain as his final contribution to a vanished era. Whatever their failings, these two great oratorios display a careful construction which combines elements of the English oratorio tradition with Wagnerism into an almost coherent, unified whole. Elgar's narrative construction when not working with accepted literary text though, is somewhat problematic. Throughout his four great choral works on Biblical themes he shows a willingness to use all the compositional and textual elements at his disposal to create dramatic and powerful works. Despite their shortcomings, the grand narrative vision of both *The Apostles* and *The Kingdom* has remained a spiritual inspiration into the 21st century.

The British choral tradition does merit additional research, particularly those compositions not written specifically for festivals and the many different descriptions of such works by their composers, the dramatic increase of oratorio composition between 1880 and 1900, and a comparison of the oratorio with the similar tradition of the secular cantata. Aesthetic questions also remain: what caused a society devoted to Handel's *Messiah* and Mendelssohn's *Elijah* to embrace three of Elgar's oratorios so wholeheartedly in the space of six years while discarding several hundred by other composers?

Taken together, the two completed oratorios of the Apostles Trilogy may be seen as effectively representing the end of an English tradition. Despite his valiant efforts, Elgar did not succeed in reviving the oratorio through these works although their effect on composers of the next generation was to be profound. He showed the way to blend orchestral and choral music in a wholly novel way by allowing both to participate appropriately. What Elgar was trying to achieve – a continuous weave of soloists, chorus and orchestra without reliance on traditional arias and recitatives – was taken to new levels of genius by Vaughan Williams, Walton and Tippett among others in the 20th century – but not as oratorios. The foundation was, however, well laid.

Elgar's cartoon of the Apostles (drawn for his nieces)

NOTES

NA   = Novello Archive
EBM   = Elgar Birthplace Museum
WCRO   = Worcester County Records Office

1   3 Jun 1903 NA
2   EBM
3   R. J. Buckley: *Sir Edward Elgar*
4   28 Jul 1904 EBM
5   15 Sep 1898 NA
6   15 Sep 1898 NA
7   Alfred Brewer: *Memories of Choirs & Cloisters*
8   14 Jun 1901 EBM
9   19 Jun 1901 EBM
10   25 Jun 1901 EBM
11   30 Jun 1901 EBM
12   2 Jul 1901 EBM
13   7 Jul 1901 EBM
14   *The Musical Times* August 1901
15   *The Musical Times* September 1901
16   6 Jul 1901 NA
17   10 Jan 1900 EBM
18   4 Mar 1900 NA
19   3 Jan 1900 EBM
20   1 Mar 1900 Alan Peake at the Royal College of Music
21   9 Oct 1900 NA
22   2 Jul 1902 Manuscript in possession of E. W. Atkins
23   31 Jul 1902 EBM
24   10 Mar 1903 EBM
25   7 Oct 1904 Malvern Gazette
26   3 Aug 1908 Letter in possession of E. W. Atkins
27   28 Oct 1902 NA

28   10 September 1903 Prefatory note on *The Apostles* – withdrawn (NA)
29   23 Oct 1903 NA
30   25 Nov 1902 NA
31   22 Dec 1902 EBM
32   2 Jan 1903 NA
33   Elgar Birthplace Museum
34   3 Feb 1903 to August Jaeger (NA)
35   25 Jun 1903 EBM
36   28 Jan 1903 NA
37   G. H. H. Hamilton: *The Art and Architecture of Russia*
38   17 Jul 1903 Elgar to Canon Gorton
39   28 Jun 1903 to August Jaeger NA
40   24 Apr 1903 NA
41   30 Jun 1903 NA
42   24 Jun 1903 EBM
43   28 Jun 1903 NA
44   30 Jun 1903 EBM
45   EBM
46   EBM
47   EBM
48   EBM
49   EBM
50   EBM
51   William Morris: *News from Nowhere and Selected Writings and Designs* (1894)
52   G. B. Shaw *William Morris* from Pen Portraits and Reviews (1931)
53   A future for English Music (1905)
54   *Letters to Nimrod* – M Kennedy
55   24 Sep 1903 (included in *Edward Elgar* by R. J. Buckley (1905)
56   *The Times* 15 Oct 1903
57   *The Daily News* 15 Oct 1903
58   *The Daily Telegraph* 15 Oct 1903

59	10 September 1903 Prefatory note on *The Apostles* – withdrawn NA	92	30 Dec 1922 EBM
		93	*The Musical Times* June 1922
60	24 Aug 1903 EBM	94	*The Musical Times* June 1922
61	16 Oct 1903 EBM	95	W. H. Reed *Elgar as I knew him* (1937)
62	6 Dec 1903 EBM		
63	6 Dec 1903 EBM	96	EMI archive
64	28 0ct 1903 NA	97	The Fifteenth Variation, Broadcast by the BBC 3 Feb 1957
65	10 Feb 1904 EBM		
66	26 October 1903 EBM	98	28 Jul 1908 NA
67	8 May 1904 Rudolf de Cordova, *The Strand*	99	Memoirs of Sir Keith Falkner (Royal College of Music)
68	6 Aug 1905 WRCO	100	W. H. Reed *Elgar as I knew him* (1937)
69	20 Sep 1905 A. J. Jaeger to Alice Elgar (EBM)		
		101	6 Dec 1907 NA
70	*The Hereford Times* 7 Oct 1905	102	28 June 1907 NA
71	*The Hereford Times* 7 Oct 1905	103	*The Musical Times* November 1957
72	29 Nov 1905	104	14 Jul 1903 NA
73	WCRO	105	Dora Penny – Elgar: Memories of a Variation (1924)
74	31 Dec 1905 EBM		
75	19 Jan 1906 NA	106	8 May 1904 Rudolf de Cordova, *The Strand*
76	2 Feb 1906 EBM		
77	EBM	107	28 Nov 1901 Birmingham Triennial Festival archives
78	21 Feb 1906 NA		
79	EBM	108	EBM
80	*The Birmingham Post* 4 Oct 1906	109	EBM
81	*The Daily Telegraph* 4 Oct 1906	110	EBM
82	*The Daily News* 4 Oct 1906	111	EBM
83	10 Oct 1906 EBM	112	10 September 1903 Prefatory note on *The Apostles* – withdrawn (NA)
84	11 Jun1907 Manuscript at Magdalen College, Cambridge		
		113	28 Jul 1903 EBM
85	EBM	114	28 Jul 1903 EBM
86	EBM	115	8 May 1904 Rudolf de Cordova, *The Strand*
87	4 Dec 1908 EBM		
88	*The Daily News* 4 Dec 1908	116	*The Musical Times* September 1923
89	*The Birmingham Daily News* 4 Dec 1908	117	4 Nov 1902 EBM
		118	EBM
90	21 Nov 1915 Leeds & District Choral Union archives	119	1 Nov 1900 NA
		120	1 Nov 1900 NA
91	8 May 1921 EBM	121	6 Nov 1969 EMI archive

122	*The Musical Times* December 1901	152	EBM
123	29 Oct 1900 NA	153	17 Aug 1903 NA
124	EBM	154	17 Sep 1903 NA
125	5 Jan 1903 EBM	155	4 Oct 1903 EBM
126	EBM	156	12 Nov 1903 NA
127	EBM	157	5 Dec 1903 NA
128	28 Jul 1903 EBM	158	5 Feb 1904 NA
129	28 Jul 1903 EBM	159	EBM
130	10 September 1903 Prefatory note on *The Apostles* – withdrawn NA	160	EBM
		161	EBM
131	10 September 1903 Prefatory note on *The Apostles* – withdrawn NA	162	EBM
		163	EBM
132	10 September 1903 Prefatory note on *The Apostles* – withdrawn NA	164	EBM
		165	EBM
133	A future for English Music (1905)	166	*The Kingdom:* An Introduction by C. V. Gorton Oct 1906 NA
134	28 Jul 1903 EBM	
135	EBM	167	EBM
136	10 September 1903 Prefatory note on *The Apostles* – withdrawn NA	168	EBM
		169	R. J. Buckley: *Edward Elgar*
137	*The Musical Times* September 1923	170	26 Jun 1906 NA
138	*The Musical Times* September 1923	171	30 Sep 1906 NA
139	*The Apostles:* An Introduction by C. V. Gorton Oct 1903 NA	172	EBM
		173	12 Aug 1906 EBM
140	10 September 1903 Prefatory note on *The Apostles* – withdrawn NA	174	23 Jul 1906 EBM
		175	28 Jan 1906 NA
141	EBM	176	2 Apr 1906 NA
142	EBM	177	3 Apr 1906 NA
143	10 September 1903 Prefatory note on *The Apostles* – withdrawn (NA)	178	16 Aug 1906 NA
		179	12 Sep 1906 EBM
144	29 Jun 1910 NA	180	*The Musical Standard* (Aug 1916)
145	12 Nov 1913 EBM	181	26 Sep 1906 EBM
146	10 September 1903 Prefatory note on *The Apostles* – withdrawn NA	182	13 Oct 1906 NA
		183	15 Jun 1907 EBM
147	EBM	184	EBM
148	EBM	185	EBM
149	3 Mar 1903 EBM	186	EBM
150	18 Mar 1906 Hallé Orchestra archive	187	EBM
		188	EBM
151	EBM	189	EBM

190   EBM
191   17 Jan 1908 EBM
192   EBM
193   EBM
194   EBM
195   EBM
196   EBM
197   EBM
198   EBM
199   EBM
200   EBM
201   EBM
202   EBM
203   EBM
204   EBM
205   EBM
206   *The Daily Telegraph* 28 Jul 1974
207   *The Musical Times* Sep 1923
208   *The Apostles:* Analytical & Descriptive
        Notes (Oct 1903) NA
209   21 Jul 1906 NA
210   C. E. McGuire

SOME PERSONALITIES IN THE STORY OF ELGAR'S APOSTLES TRILOGY

ATKINS, Sir Ivor (1869 - 1953) was Organist and Master of the Choristers at Worcester Cathedral between 1887 and 1950. He championed the music of Elgar, especially at the Three Choirs Festival, and they became life-long friends. He urged Elgar to complete the Apostles trilogy, but without success.

BREWER, Sir Alfred Herbert (1865 - 1928) was Organist and Master of the Choristers at Gloucester Cathedral between 1897 and 1928. The crisis over completing his cantata Emmaus for the 1898 Three Choirs Festival resulted in Elgar undertaking most of the orchestration. It was while Elgar's mind was engaged on this task that thoughts about the Apostles trilogy began to crystallise.

CAPEL-CURE, Edward (1869 - 1949) was an amateur cellist and composer. A curate in Worcester, he became Vicar of Bradninch in Devon and Stour Provost in Dorset. He produced a libretto for Elgar's oratorio The Light of Life and was extensively consulted by the composer about the text for the Apostles trilogy.

DAVIES, Henry Walford (1869 - 1941) was a pupil of Parry and Stanford. Elgar made representations about his work The Temple for the Three Choirs Festival in 1902. Walford Davies was organist of the Temple Church, London, for 20 years, a Professor of Music in the University of Wales and a successful broadcaster on music. He became Master of the King's Musick in succession to Elgar.

ELGAR, Caroline Alice Roberts (1848 - 1920) was born in India into a distinguished military family. Married Edward Elgar in 1889 despite opposition from her family because Elgar was a Catholic, his father in trade and his prospects and health seemed poor. Her support for Elgar enabled his genius to flower from Froissart, the concert overture written shortly after their marriage, to the Cello Concerto produced just before her death. Her diaries provide a unique insight into the composer's daily life.

EMBLETON, Henry (1854 - 1930) was a mining engineer who derived his fortune from the northern coalfields. Assistant Organist at Leeds Parish Church for a time, he became secretary and treasurer of the Leeds Choral Union. His admiration for Elgar's music led to financial subsidies for performances at the Leeds Festival. He tried to persuade Elgar to write the final oratorio of the Apostles Trilogy for many years, but without success.

GORTON, Charles Vincent (1854 - 1912) was founder of the Morecambe Competitive Festival for choirs. He asked Elgar to adjudicate in 1903. Rector of Poulton-le-Sands and Canon of Manchester Cathedral, he was an eminent theologian who advised Elgar on the librettos for The Apostles and The Kingdom.

JAEGER, August (1860 - 1909) was a native of Düsseldorf; He became Publishing Manager of Novello & Co. and quickly established a personal acquaintance that was to become a warm life-long friendship. Elgar immortalised the 'good loveable honest soul of this frail little German' in 'Nimrod', the ninth of the 'Enigma Variations'. After Jaeger's early death Elgar wrote that '[he] was for years the dear friend, the valued adviser and the stern critic of many musicians besides the writer [Elgar]; his place has been occupied but never filled'.

JOHNSTONE, George (1861 - 1932) was a Birmingham businessman and Chairman of the Orchestral Committee of the Birmingham Triennial Music Festival. His experience at dealing with composers and their problems stretched over many years with Gounod, Grieg, and Dvorak as some of the musicians he had advised over their works for the Birmingham Festival.

LITTLETON, Alfred (1845 - 1914) was Chairman of the music publishers Novello. Initially critical of Elgar's haphazard working methods and prevarications over The Apostles and The Kingdom, he actually supported Elgar through his most difficult times with the latter work. This was because August Jaeger was seriously ill and could not advise the composer as hitherto. Littleton was actually living near Elgar in Hereford by this time and the two men had become firm friends.

NEWMAN, Ernest (1869 - 1959) was born William Roberts and became a bank clerk. He changed his name when he took up musical criticism and writing on music. Elgar appreciated his gifts, although Newman was not always complimentary about Elgar's large-scale choral works. The two remained personal friends until Elgar's death.

REED, William Henry (1876 - 1942) was a violinist who helped Elgar with the construction of the Violin Concerto. Founder member of the London Symphony Orchestra in 1904 and leader from 1912. Wrote two books on Elgar and became a great friend. Tried to persuade him to complete the Apostles Trilogy without success.

REEVE, Francis (1825 - 1912) was headmaster of Littleton House, the Catholic boys' school that Elgar attended (1868 - 1872). Elgar maintained that Reeve had provided the original inspiration for the Apostles Trilogy.

STUART-WORTLEY, Alice (1862 - 1936) was the daughter of the painter Sir John Millais and second wife of Charles Stuart-Wortley (later Lord Stuart of Wortley). Hers is said to be the 'soul' enshrined in Elgar's Violin Concerto. A good amateur pianist and devoted to Elgar's music. There is evidence to suggest that Elgar was deeply in love with her to the end of his life.

COMPLETE RECORDINGS OF
'THE APOSTLES' AND 'THE KINGDOM'

THE APOSTLES, op. 49

Sheila Armstrong soprano Helen Watts contralto Robert Tear tenor
Benjamin Luxon, John Carol Case baritones Clifford Grant bass
Downe House School Choir; London Philharmonic Choir;
London Philharmonic Orchestra/Adrian Boult

(Recorded in the Kingsway Hall, London, October 1973/July 1974)

EMI CMS7 64206-2 (128 minutes)

The Gramophone — November 1988

Boult's conducting of *The Apostles* has not quite the fervour of his interpretation of *The Kingdom*, nor is the recording always as full of 'presence', but it is wonderful to have the work on CD, although owners of the original LPs will want to retain them because of the sixth side on which Sir Adrian gave an analysis of both oratorios. The faults and failings of the music have often been pointed out, and it would be idle to pretend that there are not some troughs in the level of inspiration. But, my word, the peaks! They are tremendous and deeply moving. It is in the meditative sections, where Elgar's stately sorrow flows like a river of tears, that Boult is at his most impressive and inspires the LPO and Choir to some incandescent playing and singing. His treatment of 'Turn you to the stronghold' as if it were a prayer is a piece of masterly insight and the women's choir's singing after Peter has denied Jesus is truly exquisite. The six soloists are a well-matched team, with Sheila Armstrong in radiant voice, John Carol Case a devout but mercifully unsanctimonious Jesus, and Clifford Grant, a baleful, black-voiced Judas (though his intonation is sometimes suspect). The orchestral score points the way to the symphonies and *Falstaff*, and Boult ensures that no detail is lost within the overall picture.

Alison Hargan soprano Alfreda Hodgson contralto David Rendall tenor
Stephen Roberts baritone Bryn Terfel bass-baritone Robert Lloyd bass
London Symphony Chorus; London Symphony Orchestra/Richard Hickox

(Recorded in St Jude's Church, Central Square, London NW11, March 1990)

CHAN 8875/6 (127 minutes)

The Gramophone — June 1991

Boult's 1973 EMI recording of *The Apostles* was a landmark in his career and he had to wait until he was 84 to reach it. Even then, I remember, EMI were doubtful about the whole enterprise. But perhaps the doubters had commercial nous on their side, for we have had to wait 16 years for this rival version from Chandos. Neither of Elgar's two biblical oratorios will ever be as popular as *The Dream of Gerontius* for all their glories and their special appeal to committed Elgarians; and *The Kingdom* is always likely to invite more performances than *The Apostles,* which requires six soloists and has a more diffuse structure. Nevertheless, there are episodes in *The Apostles* when Elgar was at his most inspired and inspiring.

The new recording is a very fine performance, better (in my opinion) than Hickox's *The Kingdom.* It is well recorded, with full and spacious sound in climaxes and excellent spatial effects in the final scene, with the mystic chorus properly distant yet clear and distinct (Boult used boys' voices here, which added to the ethereal quality of the music). Those who want to make comparisons between the two conductors might be interested to select four episodes. In scene 1 of Part One, in the chorus 'The Lord has chosen them', Boult is earthier, more businesslike, with more emphatic rhythm. In scene 3 of Part One, Helen Watts (Boult) is at her loveliest; Hickox's contralto, Alfreda Hodgson, sings Mary Magdalene more dramatically, but the conductor's slower tempo puts some strain on the smoothness of her phrasing and line. Boult felt that his prayer-like treatment of 'Turn you to the stronghold', the final chorus of Part One, overcame the weakness of the music. Hickox follows him and makes it even more devout and intense. The orchestral introduction to Part Two is recorded with much fuller sound by Chandos than by EMI, but the microphones are, for my taste, rather too close. Boult here is incomparable: the Elgarian elasticity and rapture flow from his baton with a spontaneity that eludes Hickox.

Where Hickox has surpassed the earlier recording is in his choice of soloists (if only his Kingdom had been as well cast). There is little to choose between his female soloists and Boult's: the soprano Alison Hargan (Chandos) is occasionally let down by her diction compared with Sheila Armstrong, but sings as beautifully and more dramatically. As I have already indicated, Watts and Hodgson are about equal.

But what counts most in *The Apostles* is the singing by the three bass soloists – and here Chandos has done Hickox proud. Bryn Terfel's St Peter is magnificent (again, if only he had sung this part in The Kingdom), Stephen Roberts is a sensitive, unsanctimonious Jesus, and Robert Lloyd's Judas is surely the very voice Elgar had in mind. On Boult's recording Clifford Grant was sadly out of form (and out of tune) and since Judas's music is the finest in the work, this was an unhappy let-down.

The singing of the London Symphony Chorus on the Chandos disc is first-rate, as is the orchestral playing. For an interpretation, stay with Boult; for a performance, then Hickox's singers carry the day.

THE KINGDOM, Op. 51

Felicity Lott, Margaret Price sopranos Yvonne Minton mezzo-soprano
Alfreda Hodgson contralto Alexander Young, Richard Morton tenors
John Shirley-Quirk, Stephen Roberts baritones
London Philharmonic Choir; London Philharmonic Orchestra/Adrian Boult

(Recorded in the Kingsway Hall, London, December 1968)

EMI CMS7 64209 2 (130 minutes)

The Gramophone – May 1988

Choices, choices . . . Of course, it's marvellous to have Boult's majestic 1968 account of *The Kingdom* restored to currency so soon, and now at mid-price, too. Sir Adrian always was a passionate admirer of this particular oratorio ('I think there is a great deal in *The Kingdom* that is more than a match for 'Gerontius', and I feel that it is a much more balanced work . . .', he writes in the introduction to this recording) and, as ever, the unaffected devotion and sheer authority of his advocacy is hard to resist. However, recent years have seen two formidable contenders emerge in the shape of Leonard Slatkin (RCA) and Richard Hickox (Chandos) and, to be perfectly honest, all three performers have so much going for them. To put matters in a rather crude nutshell: Boult enjoys the strongest team of soloists (with John Shirley-Quirk a quite outstandingly eloquent St Peter), Hickox (not surprisingly) obtains the most disciplined and full-bodied choral work, and Slatkin undoubtedly secures the finest orchestral playing – indeed, the LPO are on inspired form, responding with an exemplary sensitivity, commitment and concentration which also marked out Slatkin's magnificent account of the Second Symphony set down with this same group some 17 months later. The American also benefits from perhaps the best engineering, with Boult's

133

Kingsway Hall production now sounding just a little pale and hard-edged in comparison. Ultimately, then, the Boult must take the palm, especially with its new price advantage, though no devoted Elgarian should miss hearing Slatkin's gloriously lucid conception either.

Felicity Palmer, Margaret Marshall sopranos Arthur Davies tenor
David Wilson-Johnson baritone
London Symphony Chorus; London Symphony Orchestra/Richard Hickox

(Recorded in St Jude's Church, Central Square, London NW11, June 1989)

Chandos CHAN 8788/9 (108 minutes)

The Gramophone — February 1990

Now there are three CD versions of Elgar's last oratorio, *The Kingdom,* from which to choose . . . yet when Boult's EMI recording first appeared on LP in 1969, the likelihood of anyone else recording this work seemed remote indeed. Richard Hickox has already made a fine recording of *The Dream of Gerontius* for Chandos and seems to be working steadily through Elgar's choral works.

On the whole, I rate this 'Kingdom' below his 'Gerontius' both as interpretation and recording. The balance between choir and orchestra is far from ideal; frequently, one cannot distinguish the London Symphony Chorus's words. This is especially noticeable in the wonderful closing section of Part 3, one of the highlights of Boult's performance and very impressive, too, in Slatkin's (RCA). Here it misfires, mainly because of recording balance. The brass section in the orchestra, for example, are too prominent.

Slatkin, on the whole, is slower than Hickox. I often chide conductors for going slow in Elgar but here I feel that Hickox misses some of the music's poignancy through a desire to press on. There is an ache throughout *The Kingdom* which best manifests itself in countless passages of rubato — little hesitations and intakes of breath that Slatkin seems instinctively to comprehend as part of the texture.

I hope I don't sound too cool or dismissive about Hickox's interpretation, for that is far from my intention. Much of it is extremely fine, with a real Elgarian feel to it. He is particularly impressive and moving from 'The Breaking of the Bread' to the end of the work, and in the earlier scenes he obtains some noble singing from the chorus, while the orchestra play with both fire and sensitivity.

Which brings me to the knotty question of the soloists. They were the weak point of the Slatkin issue and they are here too. Neither quartet can compare satisfactorily with Boult's. The soprano

Margaret Marshall gives a fairly convincing account of 'The Sun Goeth Down' but betrays some strain at its dramatic climax. Arthur Davies is a good St John, Felicity Palmer an acceptable Mary Magdalene once one has come to terms with her brassy timbre. When it comes to excessive vibrato and constricted tone, there is little to choose between Luxon's St Peter (Slatkin) and David Wilson-Johnson for Hickox, except that Luxon sounds more involved emotionally.

Yvonne Kenny soprano Alfreda Hodgson mezzo-soprano Christopher Gillett tenor
Benjamin Luxon baritone London Philharmonic Choir;
London Philharmonic Orchestra/Leonard Slatkin

(Recorded in Walthamstow Town Hall, London, September/November 1987)

RCA 07863-57862-2 (116 minutes)

The Gramophone — March 1989

Boult's 1968 EMI recording of *The Kingdom* was a landmark in his life and I tend to think it was his finest achievement in the studio. He believed it was a greater work than *The Dream of Gerontius* and he interprets it with such blazing conviction that one almost agrees with him. Also, it was one of the best of the Bishop and Parker recordings and, on its transfer to CD, its sound is revealed in its full splendour. In a sense, it is incomparable and I cannot believe that any true Elgarian would wish to be without it. Having said that, nor should I wish to be without this new RCA recording conducted by the American Elgarphile, Leonard Slatkin. It is a magnificent and moving performance, brilliantly recorded and with singing and playing by the London Philharmonic Choir and Orchestra which are even finer than they provided 20 years earlier for EMI. Slatkin proves himself an Elgar conductor through and through. *The Kingdom* is like an extended slow movement, full of stately sorrow, with episodes of grandeur and exhilaration, and Slatkin understands completely how the music should be shaped and paced. He is slower, more introspective, than Boult in passages of self-communing rapture, more dramatic in the vigorous sections. Both conductors leave me in no doubt that this oratorio is a masterpiece, less flawed than its critics would have us believe. Indeed, the choral writing surpasses that in *Gerontius;* and both Slatkin and Boult make the mighty ensemble which ends Part 1 the emotional climax of the work. RCA's recording slightly favours choral sound. There is ground for sharper comparisons when it comes to the merits of the respective quartets of soloists. Margaret Price, Boult's soprano, sings 'The Sun Goeth Down' with opulent operatic splendour and tonal radiance which are not matched by Yvonne Kenny, who nevertheless brings her own devotional intensity to this lovely scena. Alfreda Hodgson (RCA) is more dramatic than Yvonne Minton (EMI), enunciates the text more meaningfully and generally gives the contralto's role unusual prominence. It is good to hear this outstanding singer so well recorded. As St John, the tenor Christopher Gillett is curiously uneven and anonymous, with a thin tone at the top, and is not in the same league as Boult's Alexander Young. But the principal solo role is that of St Peter, who must command the whole performance. Both John Shirley-Quirk (EMI) and Benjamin Luxon (RCA) do this, and the great extended solo 'Ye men of Judaea' should be the highlight of any performance. Luxon is here perhaps even more moving than Shirley-Quirk, but one cannot evade mention of the wide vibrato and 'covered' tone which are becoming inescapable features of his singing these days. They worried me a lot at first, but as the performance continued his sheer artistry won me over. He must now finish the job by recording *The Apostles*.

BIBLIOGRAPHY

PRIMARY SOURCES - MUSIC

Manuscript Material:

'The Apostles' op. 49

<u>Vocal Score:</u> British Library – Part I, with 'Turn you to the stronghold' insert marked as pp.1-25 and headed 'follow on from p.108 of v.s. proofs'
British Library – Part II, with four-page insert for Judas passage ('Let Him make speed) between rehearsal cues 154 and 156.

<u>Vocal Score complete proofs:</u> Elgar Birthplace Museum – Part I, including addition and rewriting of the Angel's part on pp. 51 - 52, addition of Mary Magdalene on top stave of p.8. '(omitted in M.S.)', reply to the engraver's feeling doubtful about the slurs on p. 94 '(So do I)'.

Elgar Birthplace Museum – Part II, with a cautious comment from John West at Novello 'Please forgive my saying anything about it' (a semitone clash between Judas and the piano part on p.49) and Elgar's 'Condoned!', expression of gratitude in Welsh to the Novello staff on p. 203, request to 'put Nobilmente if room' on p. 208.

Elgar Birthplace Museum – Parts I and II, used for making full score

Elgar Birthplace Museum – Printed vocal score with details of parts to be sung by Semi-Chorus of nine male voices to make up 12 Apostles with John, Peter and Judas.

<u>Full Score:</u> British Library with signature of Hans Richter on title page 'a true friend and an earnest admirer of the Genius who / has invented and scored this really original masterwork', names of those present at the completion of Part I scoring including A. E. Rodewald's cat 'Shover', Elgar's note about taking his 'watch to pieces', quotation from William Morris's *Earthly Paradise*

Elgar Birthplace Museum – Printed Full Score with some changes in Elgar's hand and indications of his performing practice.

<u>Libretto:</u> (Elgar's typescript for the Birmingham Festival Committee) Birmingham City Archives

'The Kingdom' op. 51

<u>Vocal Score:</u> British Library to the end of section I.
British Library to end of section III, without 'Apostles' motif in accompaniment on p.54 (added later by John Pointer of Novello), but with *Gerontius* quote in III (pp.78 - 79).

British Library sections IV – V, with keyboard layout at start of IV reminding Elgar of Humperdinck *Hansel und Gretel* Act 1 scene iii and suggestion that 'The listeners should stand during the Lord's prayer'

Elgar Birthplace Museum – Printed vocal score with Elgar's timings and suggestions for possible additions.

<u>Full Score:</u> Bodleian Library, Oxford, pp.1 - 362, with insert 176 a – d to replace *Gerontius* quote in part III.

<u>Libretto:</u> (Elgar's typescript for the Birmingham Festival Committee) Birmingham City Archives

PUBLISHED MATERIAL:

C.H. Brewer: *Emmaus* (vocal score). Novello & Co., London 1901
E. Elgar: *The Light of Life* (vocal score). Novello & Co., London 1896.
E. Elgar: *The Dream of Gerontius* (vocal score). Novello & Co., London 1900.
E. Elgar: *The Apostles* (vocal score). Novello & Co., London 1903.
E. Elgar: *The Kingdom* (vocal score). Novello & Co., London 1906.
E. Elgar: *The Light of Life* (full score). Edited by R. Anderson and J.N. Moore. Elgar Complete Edition vol. 3, Novello & Co., London 1981.
E. Elgar: *The Dream of Gerontius* (full score). Edited by C. Kent and J. N. Moore. Elgar Complete Edition vol. 6, Novello & Co., London 1982.
E. Elgar: *The Apostles* (full score). Edited by R. Anderson and C. Kent. Elgar Complete Edition vol. 8, Novello & Co., London 1983.
E. Elgar: *The Kingdom* (full score). Edited by R. Anderson and C. Kent. Elgar Complete Edition vol. 9, Novello & Co., London 1984.
E. Elgar: *The Spanish Lady* Realised and Edited by P. M. Young. Novello & Co., London 1995
E. Elgar: Symphony no. 3. Realised by A. Payne. Boosey & Hawkes London 1997
C. Saint-Saens: *The Promised Land*. Novello & Co., London 1913.

BIBLIOGRAPHY

PRIMARY SOURCES – DOCUMENTS

British Library: Add MS 47900 A *(Lux Christi)*; Add MS 47902 *(The Dream of Gerontius)*; Add MS 47904 A *(The Apostles)*; BL Add MS 47904 B *(The Apostles)*; BL Add MS 47905 A *(The Kingdom)*, BL Add MS 47905 B *(The Kingdom)*, BL Add MS 47906 *(The Last Judgement)*.

E. Elgar: *My Friends Pictured Within: the Subjects of the Enigma Variations as Portrayed in Contemporary Photographs and Elgar's Manuscript.* Novello & Co., London [c1948]

E. Elgar: *Letters to Nimrod.* Edited by P. M. Young. Denis Dobson, London 1965.

E. Elgar: *A Future for English Music.* Edited by P. M. Young. Forward by A. Lewis. Denis Dobson, London 1968.

E. Elgar: *Elgar and His Publishers: Letters of a Creative Life.* Edited by J. N. Moore. Clarendon Press, Oxford 1987

E. Elgar: *The Windflower Letters: Correspondence with Alice Caroline Stuart-Wortley and Her Family.* Edited by J. N. Moore. Clarendon Press, Oxford 1989.

E. Elgar: *Edward Elgar: Letters of a Lifetime.* Selected and edited by J. N. Moore. Clarendon Press, Oxford 1990.

C. V. Gorton: *The Apostles: an Interpretation of the Libretto.* Novello & Co., London 1903.

C. V. Gorton: *The Kingdom: an Interpretation of the Libretto.* Novello & Co., London 1906.

A. J. Jaeger: *The Dream of Gerontius: Book of Words with Analytical and Descriptive Notes.* Novello & Co, London 1901 Reprint, 1974.

A. J. Jaeger: *The Apostles: Book of Words with Analytical Notes and Descriptive Notes.* Novello & Co., London 1903.

A. J. Jaeger: *The Kingdom: Book of Words with Analytical Notes and Descriptive Notes.* Novello & Co., London 1906.

Joseph Moore Papers. City of Birmingham Archives.

Papers of Frederick R. Spark. Leeds County Archives.

SECONDARY SOURCES

W. E. Addis and T. Arnold: *A Catholic Dictionary.* Revised with additions by T. B. Schanell. Sixth edition. Kegan Paul, Trench, Trübner and Co. Ltd., London 1903.

K. Allen: *August Jaeger: Portrait of Nimrod. A Life in Letters and Other Writings.* Scolar Press, Aldershot 2000.

J. Allison: *Edward Elgar – Sacred Music.* Seren, Bridgend 1994

R. Anderson: 'Elgar and Some Apostolic Problems'. The Musical Times. January 1984

R. Anderson: *Elgar in Manuscript.* British Library, London 1990.

R. Anderson: *Elgar.* Maxwell Macmillan International, New York 1993.

W. R. Anderson: *Introduction to the Music of Elgar.* Dobson, London 1949.

*The Apocrypha**

E. W. Atkins: *The Elgar-Atkins Friendship.* David & Charles, Newton Abbot c1984.

N. Barton: 'Oratorios and Cantatas'. In *Music in Britain: The Romantic Age,* edited by N. Temperly, pp. 214-241. The Athlone Press, London 1981.

E. A. Baughan: "'The Apostles' and 'Elgar's Future'". In Music and Musicians. John Lane, The Bodley Head, London 1906

L. Beckett: *Richard Wagner: Parsifal.* Cambridge University Press, 1981.

The Best of Me: A Gerontius Centenary Companion. Edited by G. Hodgkins: Elgar Editions, Rickmansworth 1999.

A. Boden, *Three Choirs: A History of the Festival.* Alan Sutton, Stroud 1992.

R. Boughton: *The Death and Resurrection of the Music Festival.* William Reeves, London 1913.

A. Boult: 'Composer as Conductor'. In Elgar Centenary Sketches, Novello & Co., London 1957.

W. Bousset: *The Antichrist Legend.* London 1896. *

A. H. Brewer: *Memories of Choirs and Cloisters.* London: John Lane, 1931.

R. J. Buckley: *Sir Edward Elgar.* J. Lane, London 1905.

R. Burley and F. C. Carruthers: *Edward Elgar: The Record of A Friendship.* Barrie & Jenkins, London 1972.

H. A. Chambers: *Edward Elgar Centenary Sketches.* Novello & Co., London 1957.

R. H. Charles: *Lectures on the Apocalypse.* Oxford 1896 and 1922. *

Choral Music on Record. Edited by A. Blyth. Cambridge University Press, 1991.

F. L. Cohen: 'Music in the Synagogue'. The Musical Times, September 1899

F. L. Cohen: 'Song in the Synagogue'. The Musical Times, August 1899

D. Cooke: *I Saw the World End. A Study of Wagner's Ring.* Oxford University Press, 1979.

S. R. Craggs: *Edward Elgar: A Source Book.* Scolar Press, Aldershot 1995.

A. Cruden: *A Complete Concordance to the Old and New Testament.* Burns and Oates, London 1885.

J. S. Curwen: *Memorials of John Curwen.* J. Curwen & Sons, London 1882.

E. L. Cutts: *A Handy Book of the Church of England.* London, 1901.

C. Dahlhaus: *Richard Wagner's Music Dramas.* Translated by M. Whitall. Cambridge University Press, 1992.

E. Day: 'Interpreting Gerontius', in The Musical Times, June 1969

P. Dennison: 'Elgar and Wagner'. Music and Letters LVI, no. 2 1985

M. De-la-Noy: *Elgar, the Man.* A. Lane, London 1983.

A. E. F. Dickinson: 'The Drama Behind Elgar's Music', in Music and Letters XXXIII, no. 2 April 1942

T. F. Dunhill: *Sir Edward Elgar.* Blackie & Son Ltd., London 1938.

T. F. Dunhill: *Portrait of Elgar.* Oxford University Press, 1968

Elgar Centenary Sketches. Edited by H. A. Chambers, Novello & Company Ltd., London 1957.

Encyclopaedia Britannica

F. W. Farrar: *The Early Days of Christianity.* London 1905. *

L. Foreman: 'The Revival of Elgar's Choral Music'. Musical Opinion January 1975

C. Forsyth: *Music and Nationalism.* Macmillan, London 1911.

H. Foss: 'Elgar and His Age'. Music and Letters XVI, no. 1 January 1935;
(Elgar Commemorative Issue)

W. Frankland: *The Early Eucharist* London, 1902. *

C. V. Gorton: *The Apostles: Sacred Oratorio by Edward Elgar. An Interpretation of the Libretto.*
Novello & Company, Ltd., London 1903

C. V. Gorton: *The Kingdom: Sacred Oratorio by Edward Elgar. An Interpretation of the Libretto.*
Novello & Company Ltd., London 1906

C. Grogan: 'Elgar's Rejected Apostle'. The Musical Times February 1988

C. Grogan: 'A Study of Elgar's Creative Process in The Apostles (Op. 49), with particular
reference to Sc.II 'By the Wayside'. Ph.D. dissertation, University of London, Royal Holloway &
Bedford New College, 1989.

C. Grogan: 'My Dear Analyst': Some Observations on Elgar's Correspondence with A. J. Jaeger
regarding The Apostles Project'. Music and Letters, 72, no. 1 February 1991

J. Hamilton-Patterson: *Gerontius.* Vintage, London 1990

A. Hillard: *Life of Christ in the Words of the Four Gospels.* London, 1894 **

G. Hodgkins: *Providence and Art: a Study in Elgar's Religious Beliefs.* Elgar Society, London 1979

G. Hodgkins: 'Elgar: A Bibliography'. The Music Review 54, no. 1 February 1993

J. Holbrooke: *Contemporary British Composers.* Cecil Palmer, London 1925.

Holy Bible. Oxford, 1899 *

F. Howes: *The English Musical Renaissance.* Secker & Warburg, London 1966.

D. Hunt: *Elgar and the Three Choirs Festival.* Osborne Books, Worcester 1999.

A. J. Jaeger: *The Dream of Gerontius: Book of Words with Analytical and Descriptive Notes.*
Novello & Co., London 1900 (reprinted 1974).

A. J. Jaeger: *The Apostles: Book of Words with Analytical Notes and Descriptive Notes.* Novello & Co.,
London 1903.

A. J. Jaeger: *The Kingdom: Book of Words with Analytical Notes and Descriptive Notes.* Novello & Co.,
London 1906.

Rev. A. C. Jennings and Rev. W. H. Lowe: *The Psalms, with Introductions and Critical Notes.*
Second edition, revised. Macmillan and Co., London 1885.

E. Jose: *The Significance of Elgar.* Cantor, London 1934.

W. Kearns: 'Horatio, Parker, Edward Elgar and Choral Music at the Turn of the Century'.
The Elgar Society Journal 10, no. 1 March 1997

H. Kelly: *A History of the Church of Christ* vol.1 (London, 1901). *

M. Kennedy: *Portrait of Elgar.* Clarendon Press, Oxford 1993.

I. Ker: *John Henry Newman: A Biography.* Clarendon Press, Oxford 1988.

W. Klassen: *Judas – Betrayer or Friend of Jesus?* SCM Press, London 1996

J. Knowles: *Elgar's Interpreters on Record: an Elgar Discography.* 2nd ed. Thames Publishing, London 1985.

H. Latham: *Pastor pastorum.* Deighton Bell, Cambridge 1902. *

Letters and Diaries of John Henry Newman Edited by C. Dessain et. al. Oxford University Press, 1961-84.

The Liverpool Bible *

H. W. Longfellow: 'The Divine Tragedy'. In *The Works of Henry Wadsworth Longfellow.* Wordsworth Editions Ltd., Ware 1994

The Luther Bible: Translated by W. A. Ellis. Kegan Paul, Trench, Trübner & Co., London 1893

B. Maine: *Elgar, His Life and Works.* Bell, London 1933.

John Masefield: *The Trial of Jesus.* William Heinemann, London 1925

C. E. McGuire: 'Elgar, Judas and the Theology of Betrayal'. 19th-Century Music XXIII 2000

C. E McGuire: *Elgar's Oratorios – The Creation of an Epic Narrative.* Scolar Press, Aldershot 2002

W. McNaught: *Elgar.* Novello & Co., London 1960.

D. M. McVeagh: *Edward Elgar: His Life and Music.* J. M. Dent & Sons, Ltd., London 1955.

H. Maccoby: *Judas Iscariot and the Myth of Jewish Evil.* The Free Press, New York 1992

B. Mohn: 'Personifying the Saviour? English oratorio representation of the words of Christ'. In Nineteenth-Century British Music Studies. Volume 1, edited by Bennett Zon, Scolar Press, Aldershot 1999.

R. Monk (Editor): *Edward Elgar – Music and Literature.* Scolar Press, Aldershot 1993

R. Monk (Editor): *Elgar Studies.* Scolar Press, Aldershot 1990

J. N. Moore: *Elgar on Record: the Composer and the Gramophone.* EMI Records, London 1974.

J. N. Moore: *Edward Elgar: a Creative Life.* Oxford University Press, 1984.

F. Moretti: *The Modern Epic.* Translated by Q. Hoare. Verso, London 1996.

M. Musgrave: *The Musical Life of the Crystal Palace.* Cambridge University Press, 1995.

Music in Britain: The Romantic Age, 1800 - 1914. Edited by N. Temperly. The Athlone Press, London 1981.

R. Nettel: *Music in the Five Towns, 1840 - 1914.* Oxford University Press, 1944.

J. New: *Traditional aspects of Hell* Cambridge, 1907 *

E. Newman: 'The Music Makers by Edward Elgar'. The Musical Times, September 1912

E. Newman: 'The Spirit of England: Edward Elgar's New Choral Work'. The Musical Times, May 1916

E. Newman: 'Elgar's Fourth of August'. The Musical Times, July 1917

E. Newman: *Elgar.* Third edition. J. Lane, The Bodley Head Ltd., London 1922.

J. H. Newman: *The Dream of Gerontius.* Burns and Oates, London 1865

J. H. Newman: *Letters and Diaries of John Henry Newman.* Edited by C. Dessain et al Oxford University Press, 1961-84.

T. Page and A. Walpole: *The Acts of the Apostles* London, 1902. *

I. Parrott: *Elgar.* Dent, London 1971.

C. H. H. Parry: 'Leit-Motif. In *A Dictionary of Music and Musicians,* edited by J. A. Fuller Maitland. Macmillan and Co., Ltd., London 1906.

M. Parsons: *A Prevailing Passion: A History of Worcester Festival Choral Society.* Osborne Heritage, Worcester 1996.

A. W. Patterson: *The Story of the Oratorio.* The Walter Scott Publishing Co. Ltd., London 1902.

E. Pauer: *Traditional Hebrew Melodies.* Preface by F. L. Cohen. Augner and Co., London undated

W. Pinnock: *An Analysis of New Testament History.* Cambridge 1894. *

J. F. Porte: *Sir Edward Elgar.* Kegan Paul, London 1921.

J. F. Porte: *Elgar and His Music: an Appreciative Study.* Pitman, London 1933.

Mrs. R. Powell: (nèe Dora Penny): 'The Words of The Apostles and The Kingdom'. The Musical Times, July 1948 and May 1949

Mrs. R. Powell (nèe Dora Penny): 'The First Performances of The Apostles and The Kingdom'. The Musical Times 1960

Mrs. R. Powell (nèe Dora Penny): *Edward Elgar: Memories of a Variation.* Revised and edited by C. Powell, with an addendum by J. N. Moore. Scolar Press, Aldershot 1994

B. Rainbow: *John Curwen: A Short Biography.* Novello & Co., London 1980.

Red Letter New Testament *

W. H. Reed: *Elgar as I Knew Him.* Oxford University Press (Gollancz), 1936.

W. H. Reed: *Elgar.* J. M. Dent, London 1939.

E. Renan: *Antichrist,* London, 1904 *

E. Renan: *The Apostles,* London, 1895. **

E. Robinson: *A Harmony of the Four Gospels.* Revised edition, with footnotes from the revised version of 1881 and additional notes by M. B. Riddle. The Riverside Press, Cambridge 1886. *

G. Rowell: 'The Anglican Tradition from the Reformation to the Oxford Movement'. In *Confession and Absolution* (edited by M. Dudley and G. Rowell). SPCK, London 1990.

P. A. Scholes: *The Puritans and Music in England and New England.* Oxford University Press, 1934.

P. A. Scholes: *The Mirror of Music, 1844 - 1944.* Oxford University Press, 1947.

R. Sharrock: 'Newman's Poetry'. In *Newman after a Hundred Years.* Edited by I. Ker and A. G. Hill, Oxford University Press, 1990.

G. B. Shaw: *Shaw's Music: The Complete Musical Criticism of Bernard Shaw.* Second revised edition; edited by D. H. Lawrence. The Bodley Head, London 1981,

D. Smith: *The Art of Preaching.* Hodder and Stoughton, London 1906.

J. S. Smith: *The Story of Music in Birmingham.* Cornish Brothers Ltd., Birmingham 1945

J. Sprittles: 'Leeds Musical Festivals'. Publications of the Thoresby Society: Miscellany 13, part 2, No. 108, 1960

R. A. Stradling and M. Hughes: *The English Musical Renaissance 1860-1940: Construction and Deconstruction.* Routledge, London 1993.

The Topical Bible: Oxford University Press, 1892 *

M. Turner: *The Literary Mind.* Oxford: Oxford University Press, 1996.

C. Vaughan, *The Church of the First Days* vols. 1-3 (London and Cambridge, 1865, 1866, 1866).*

R. Wagner: *Richard Wagner's Complete Prose Works.* Edited by W. A. Ellis: Kegan Paul, Trench, Trübner & Co., London 1899.

W. Wake and N. Lardner: *The Apocryphal New Testament**

R. Wagner: *Opera and Drama.* Translated by W. A. Ellis. Kegan Paul, Trench, Trübner & Co., London 1893

E. Walker: *A History of Music in England.* Clarendon Press, Oxford 1907.

R. Whatley: *Lectures on the Characters of Our Lord's Apostles and Especially their Conduct at the Time of His Apprehension and Trial.* John W. Parker and Son, London 1859 and 1893*

D. Whitby: Additional Annotations to the New & Old Testaments Kegan Paul, Trench, Trübner & Co., London 1901

P. M. Young: *Elgar, O.M: a Study of a Musician.* Collins, London 1955.

P. M. Young: 'John Henry Newman, Edward Elgar and The Dream of Gerontius'. Occasional Paper No. 1, The University of Birmingham, Institute for Advanced Research in the Humanities, 1991.

P. M. Young: *Elgar, Newman and The Dream of Gerontius: In the Tradition of English Catholicism.* Scholar Press, Aldershot 1995.

*   including Elgar's own copy (at the Elgar Birthplace Museum)

**   including Elgar's own copy (in the British Library)